Best of Bridge

Everyday Celebrations

Everyday Celebrations

125 Recipes for Friends & Family

Robert
ROSE

For complete cataloguing information, see page 244.

Disclaimer
The recipes in this book have been carefully tested by our kitchen and
our tasters. To the best of our knowledge, they are safe and nutritious
for ordinary use and users. For those people with food or other allergies,
or who have special food requirements or health issues, please read the
suggested contents of each recipe carefully and determine whether or
not they may create a problem for you. All recipes are used at the risk
of the consumer.

We cannot be responsible for any hazards, loss or damage that may
occur as a result of any recipe use.

For those with special needs, allergies, requirements or health problems,
in the event of any doubt, please contact your medical adviser prior to
the use of any recipe.

DESIGN AND PRODUCTION: Kevin Cockburn/PageWave Graphics Inc.
EDITOR: Kathleen Fraser
INDEXER: Gillian Watts
PHOTOGRAPHY, FOOD & PROP STYLING: Ashley Lima
PHOTOGRAPHY ASSISTANT: Katie Tenenbaum
ICONS: © Getty Images

COVER IMAGE: Hearty Ragu Pappardelle (page 114)

The publisher gratefully acknowledges the financial support of our
publishing program by the Government of Canada through the
Canada Book Fund.

Canadä

Published by Robert Rose Inc.
120 Eglinton Avenue East, Suite 800, Toronto, Ontario, Canada M4P 1E2
Tel: (416) 322-6552 Fax: (416) 322-6936
www.robertrose.ca

Printed and bound in China

1 2 3 4 5 6 7 8 9 ESP 30 29 28 27 26 25 24 23 22

CONTENTS

~

INTRODUCTION

Sharing food with family and friends is truly a celebration, and if the past couple of years have taught us anything, it is that those times when we can share a meal made with love together have a very special place in our hearts. Although distance can keep us apart, many try to stay in touch and celebrate by sharing recipes, and dropping off a meal or baked goods to tuck away in the freezer. These little celebrations of daily life and support can mean a lot. There will always be big celebrations — holidays, birthdays, anniversaries — and even greeting card holidays as some refer to them (Valentine's Day), but the small everyday accomplishments we get through are the ones we also want to enjoy with family and friends.

There are so many reasons to celebrate. Sometimes it's a birthday or a celebration of life for a person loved and often thought of, so you make their favorites or their signature dishes. Other times you are putting together a charcuterie antipasto board and just want to hang out with some friends. Or maybe you've made a seasonal dessert with fresh strawberries you just picked and spontaneously invite the neighbors over. It's a moment in time, a snapshot that can be enjoyed, savored and remembered with those you love around you. We may have photos to help us remember these times, but we also have recipes with familiar tastes and aromas that evoke shared memories, so everyone can recall the reason for that celebration gathering long after.

Cooking everyday can feel like a chore, but for many of us it provides a release of energy and a way to show our love for family and friends. What if we looked at each meal or recipe we prepared as a celebration in its own right? What if we thought about the small things, the little things that can occur every day, and made those a celebration? Let's think about going to the grocery store, gathering those ingredients, even following a new recipe, as a reason to celebrate.

Each day that passes, we may not get a chance to stop and think there's a reason to celebrate or prepare a special dinner, beverage or sweet treat. But what if we changed that and made more of the little things matter? We (Sylvia and Emily) both have reasons to celebrate each day! So do the Best of Bridge readers, and in this cookbook, you may read big and small stories of how we include food to celebrate.

Let's think back to a time when favorite recipes were shared and handed down by family members for the younger generations to recreate in their own kitchens for their own families. Sharing the love of food and families is something that Best of Bridge has done since its inception and continues to do today. We can't even tell you all our favorites in this book, as there are just too many that are reminders of wonderfully good times we have shared with loved ones. We hope that the recipes will become ways for you to celebrate each day as well!

Please share your everyday celebrations with us. We would love to see what you're cooking from Best of Bridge, so do post your photos of recipes you've shared with family and friends. And tag us on Instagram @BestofBridge and on Facebook so we can celebrate along with you!

Make every day a celebration!
All our love,
Sylvia and Emily

GUIDE TO RECIPE ICONS

 MAKE AHEAD: Recipes that can be prepared in advance, including recipes that can be made ahead in stages to cook later

 5 INGREDIENTS OR FEWER: Recipes that use five main ingredients or fewer, not including water, oils, salt and black pepper

 30 MINUTES OR LESS: Recipes that can be prepared from start to finish in 30 minutes or less

 SHEET PAN: Recipes that are cooked on a sheet pan and baked in the oven

 ONE SKILLET/POT MEAL: Recipes that require only one pot or one skillet to cook

 GRILLING: Recipes that are cooked on a charcoal or gas grill

 VEGETARIAN: Recipe ingredients do not include meat or fish products but can include dairy, eggs and honey.

 GLUTEN FREE: Recipe ingredients do not contain any gluten, which is protein found in wheat and other grains such as barley and rye. (Please read labels for ingredients when cooking at home to ensure no wheat products have been used.)

BREAKFAST AND BRUNCH

~

POTATO NUGGET BREAKFAST CASSEROLE

SERVES 6 TO 8 ·

Who says these fun-to-eat potato puffs are just for kids? This classic layered breakfast is also delicious for lunch or dinner. If you want a few more minutes to sleep, prepare this the night before and pop it in the oven in the morning.

1 lb (500 g) bulk spicy or mild Italian sausage

1 small onion, finely chopped

1 red bell pepper, finely chopped

2 tsp (10 mL) dried Italian seasoning

6 large eggs

1/4 (60 mL) cup milk

1 1/2 (375 mL) cup shredded sharp (old) Cheddar cheese or jalapeño Jack cheese, divided

1 1/2 lbs (750 g) frozen potato nuggets or potato puffs (about 7 cups/1.75 L)

1 green onion, thinly sliced

1 Preheat oven to 350°F (180°C). Lightly grease a 13- by 9-inch (33 by 23 cm) baking dish; set aside. In a large skillet, over medium-high heat, add sausage, onion, red pepper and Italian seasoning. Cook, breaking up meat into small chunks, about 7 to 10 minutes, until meat is cooked through. Transfer mixture to prepared dish, spread in an even layer; let cool 5 minutes.

2 Meanwhile, in a bowl, whisk together eggs and milk; pour over sausage mixture. Sprinkle on half of the cheese, then arrange potatoes in a single layer on top. Bake 35 minutes or until egg is set.

3 Remove from oven and set oven to broil. Sprinkle remaining cheese and the green onion over top; broil 2 to 3 minutes or until cheese is light golden brown. Cool slightly before serving.

MAKE AHEAD

The casserole can be assembled the night before; cover and refrigerate. The next morning, remove from refrigerator and uncover before preheating oven. Bake as directed.

TIP

For a vegetarian version, swap out the sausage with plant-based sausage.

BREAKFAST BURRITO FOR TWO

SERVES 2 · · :30

When you have a quiet breakfast for two, it can be
a very special morning. Emily's friend Donna's children
request this on repeat, so you may have to double it
if you have to share with more than two!

4 breakfast sausages,
casings removed

2 large whole wheat
flour tortillas (about
10 inches/25 cm each)

1 cup (250 mL) leftover
scrambled eggs (see Tip)

2 slices cooked bacon

$\frac{1}{2}$ cup (125 mL) mild salsa

$\frac{1}{4}$ cup (60 mL) shredded
Cheddar cheese

2 tbsp (30 mL) cooked
beans (optional)

1 tbsp (15 mL) sliced green
onion (optional)

$\frac{1}{2}$ ripe avocado, sliced

Pinch each salt and black
pepper

Pinch smoked paprika

Sour cream, hot sauce
(optional)

1 In a large skillet over medium heat, crumble in
sausages and cook, stirring to break up meat until
no longer pink. Scrape onto paper towel lined plate.

2 Preheat oven to 425°F (220°C). Line a small baking
sheet with parchment paper.

3 Lay tortillas onto flat work surface and divide eggs
in half, on center of each. Top each with bacon
and cooked sausage and salsa. Sprinkle each with
cheese, beans and onion, if using, and top with
avocado. Sprinkle with salt, pepper and smoked
paprika. Fold in sides and end of the tortilla and roll
up. Wrap each in foil and place on prepared pan.
Bake for about 10 minutes or until cheese is melted.

4 Serve with sour cream and hot sauce, if using.

MAKE AHEAD

Wrap the burritos and refrigerate up to 2 days.
Add about 5 minutes to the oven time when
warming up.

TIPS

TO MAKE SCRAMBLED EGGS: In a bowl, whisk 3 large
eggs with a pinch of salt and black pepper. Heat a
little butter or oil in a small nonstick skillet and pour
in eggs. Cook, stirring gently for about 2 minutes or
until fluffy and just cooked through.

Breakfast sausages can come in different sizes, so
if your sausages are a bit on the large size you will
only need two for the recipe.

This is a great recipe to use up any leftover beans
you have around, like black beans, white beans,
baked beans or even chickpeas!

EGGS BENEDICT STRATA WITH HOLLANDAISE

SERVES 8 TO 10 ·

We have tried to make eggs Benedict for a crowd, and it can be hard to keep everything hot enough to serve without it getting dried out. So simplify your life and serve this strata. While it bakes, you can whip up the hollandaise sauce.

STRATA

8 English muffins

6 oz (180 g) sliced Black Forest ham, chopped

1 cup (250 mL) shredded Gruyère, Cheddar or Swiss cheese

8 large eggs

1 cup (250 mL) light (5%) cream

2/3 cup (150 mL) milk

3 tbsp (45 mL) chopped fresh chives or green onions

1 tbsp (15 mL) Dijon mustard

1/4 tsp (1 mL) black pepper

HOLLANDAISE SAUCE

3 tbsp (45 mL) water

3 large egg yolks

1/4 tsp (1 mL) each salt and black pepper

2/3 cup (150 mL) unsalted butter, melted and cooled

1 tbsp (15 mL) lemon juice

2 tbsp (10 mL) chopped fresh dill (optional)

1. STRATA: Grease a 13- x 9-inch (33 by 23 cm) baking dish. Open English muffins and place half into prepared dish. Sprinkle with ham and cheese. Top with remaining English muffin halves, cut side up.

2. In a large bowl, whisk together eggs, cream, milk, chives, mustard and pepper. Pour over ham and English muffin layers. Cover and refrigerate for at least 4 hours or up to 24 hours.

3. Preheat oven to 375°F (190°C). Uncover baking dish and, using a spatula, press down muffins gently into custard. Bake for about 45 minutes or until golden and knife inserted in center comes out clean.

4. HOLLANDAISE: Meanwhile, in top of double boiler or heatproof bowl, whisk water and egg yolks together with salt and pepper for 30 seconds or until pale yellow and frothy. Whisk mixture for 3 minutes or until ribbons form. Remove pan from heat; whisk in butter, 1 tbsp (15 mL) at a time, until sauce begins to thicken. Still whisking, pour remaining butter into sauce in slow steady stream. Stir in lemon juice and dill (if using). Remove from heat and spoon onto strata when serving.

VARIATION

Substitute smoked turkey or leftover cooked turkey for the ham.

TIP

The remaining egg whites can be used to make meringue, add to an omelet or for another baking project.

SHEET-PAN MUSHROOM AND HAM FRITTATA

SERVES 12 · 🍳 · ▨

Here's a great dish to serve a crowd during the holidays. Everyone gets to enjoy the frittata at the same time since it's baked on a sheet pan. Serve with a side of toast or roasted potatoes. Or enjoy slices in a bun, English muffin, biscuit or bagel.

2 tbsp (30 mL) butter

8 oz (250 g) sliced mushrooms (about 3 cups/750 mL)

1/2 tsp (2 mL) salt

4 cups (1 L) lightly packed baby spinach, roughly chopped

2 cups (500 mL) chopped cooked ham

1/4 cup (60 mL) chopped sun-dried tomatoes in oil, drained

3 green onions, sliced

2 tsp (10 mL) dried Italian seasoning

1 tsp (5 mL) black pepper

12 large eggs

1/4 cup (60 mL) milk

3/4 cup (175 mL) grated Parmesan cheese

1 Preheat oven to 350°F (180°C). Coat a rimmed baking sheet with cooking spray or line with parchment paper.

2 In a large skillet, over medium-high heat, melt butter and add mushrooms and salt; cook, stirring occasionally, for 6 minutes, until most of the liquid has evaporated from the mushrooms. Stir in spinach, ham, sun-dried tomatoes, green onions, Italian seasoning and pepper; continue cooking for about 2 minutes, stirring constantly.

3 Transfer mixture to prepared baking sheet and spread in an even layer. In a large bowl, whisk together eggs and milk; gently pour over filling. Sprinkle top with cheese and carefully transfer to oven. Bake for 20 to 25 minutes or until eggs are set in the center. Let cool slightly before serving.

VARIATION
Substitute ham with cooked and crumbled sausage or leftover meat from a previous meal.

MAKE AHEAD
Make up to 2 days ahead. Can be served cold or warm. To reheat, wrap each serving in paper towel and microwave on high for 30 to 60 seconds.

BRAN SCONES

SERVES 8 · · · ·

These flaky and tender scones are quick to prepare for breakfast, brunch or tea time. You can mix and refrigerate the dry ingredients in advance, so it's ready to go when you start baking. They are especially tasty slathered with our delicious Raspberry Maple Butter, on page 31.

2 cups (500 mL) all-purpose flour

1/2 cup (125 mL) wheat bran

1/4 cup (60 mL) packed brown sugar

1 tbsp (15 mL) baking powder

1/2 tsp (2 mL) baking soda

1/4 tsp (1 mL) salt

1/2 cup (125 mL) cold butter

3/4 cup (175 mL) buttermilk

1 large egg

1 tbsp (15 mL) coarse sugar (see Tip)

1 Preheat oven to 425°F (220°C); set aside a lightly greased or parchment paper lined baking sheet.

2 In a large bowl, whisk together flour, bran, brown sugar, baking powder, baking soda and salt. Using a cheese grater, grate the butter into the dry ingredients; toss to mix so butter is evenly coated. In a small bowl, whisk together the buttermilk and egg and add all but 2 tsp (10 mL) of liquid to dry ingredients; stir until mixture just comes together.

3 Gather the dough into a ball. On a lightly floured surface, pat dough into a rectangle, about 1/2 inch (1 cm) thick. Fold it into thirds over itself, then pat the dough into a rectangle, about 1 inch (2.5 cm) thick and cut into 8 squares.

4 Transfer to prepared baking sheet and brush tops with remaining buttermilk mixture; sprinkle with coarse sugar. Bake 15 to 20 minutes, until golden brown. Transfer to a wire rack to cool.

VARIATION

Add 1/2 cup (125 mL) raisins or dried cranberries.

TIPS

Store in an airtight container for up to 2 days or freeze in an airtight freezer container for up to 2 weeks.

Coarse sugar options include sanding, turbinado, muscovado and Demerara. These add a touch of sweetness and crunch.

APPLE CINNAMON MUFFIN WITH CRUMBLE

MAKES 12 MUFFINS · · ·

This is just a really good muffin recipe to start the day off right. Make it gluten-free simply by using your favorite cup-for-cup gluten free-flour. Emily's friend Lisa's gluten-free family members call this recipe "a definite keeper."

CRUMBLE TOPPING

1/3 cup (75 mL) all-purpose flour

3 tbsp (45 mL) packed light brown sugar

1/2 tsp (2 mL) ground cinnamon

2 tbsp (30 mL) canola oil

APPLE CINNAMON MUFFINS

2 cups (500 mL) all-purpose flour

1 tbsp (15 mL) ground cinnamon

1 tbsp (15 mL) baking powder

1 tsp (5 mL) baking soda

1/2 tsp (2 mL) salt

1 cup (250 mL) packed light brown sugar

1/2 cup (125 mL) canola oil

2 large eggs

1 cup (250 mL) buttermilk

1 tsp (5 mL) vanilla

1 cup (250 mL) diced apples

1 TOPPING: In a small bowl, combine flour, sugar and cinnamon. Add oil and, using a fork, mash into flour mixture until crumbly. Set aside.

2 Preheat oven to 425°F (225°C). Grease or spray 12 muffin cups well; set aside.

3 APPLE CINNAMON MUFFINS: In a bowl, whisk together flour, cinnamon, baking powder, baking soda and salt. In another bowl, whisk together sugar, oil and eggs until well combined. Whisk in buttermilk and vanilla. Stir flour mixture into butter mixture until combined. Stir in apples and scoop into prepared pan. Sprinkle crumble topping over tops of all the muffins and press topping gently.

4 Bake for 5 minutes. Reduce oven to 375°F (190°C) and bake for about 10 minutes or until tester inserted in center comes out clean. Let cool completely.

TIPS

Wrap muffins individually and freeze in airtight container for up to 2 weeks.

Muffin tins can vary in size. If you have a smaller volume (around 1/4 cup/60 mL), you will fill them to overflowing or simply make more muffins (up to 18). Newer muffins tins can be larger to accommodate these large bakery-style muffins.

CINNAMON RAISIN LOAF

MAKES 10 TO 12 SLICES · · 🌱

Get your day off to a tasty start. This tender quick bread has plenty of raisins in every bite, plus whole wheat flour adds a nutty flavor that pairs well with the spices. Any leftover slices are wonderful toasted the next day.

1¼ (300 mL) cups all-purpose flour

¾ cup (175 mL) whole wheat flour

1½ tsp (7 mL) ground cinnamon

1½ tsp (7 mL) baking powder

½ tsp (2 mL) baking soda

½ tsp (2 mL) salt

¼ tsp (1 mL) ground cloves

Pinch grated nutmeg

2 large eggs

1 cup (250 mL) granulated sugar

1 cup (250 mL) sour cream

½ cup (125 mL) canola oil

1¼ cup (300 mL) raisins

1 Preheat oven to 375°F (190°C). Line a 9- by 5-inch (23 by 12.5 cm) loaf pan with parchment paper and lightly spray with nonstick cooking spray. In a medium bowl, whisk together all-purpose flour, whole wheat flour, cinnamon, baking powder, baking soda, salt, cloves and nutmeg. In a large bowl, whisk together eggs, sugar, sour cream and oil. Add flour mixture and stir to moisten. Add raisins and stir until just combined. Scrape into prepared loaf pan.

2 Bake for 1 hour, until a tester inserted in the center comes out clean. Let cool in pan on a wire rack for 10 minutes, then transfer loaf to a wire rack to cool completely.

TIPS

If the raisins are very dry, give them a quick soak in hot water for 10 minutes; drain well before using.

Store in an airtight container for up to 3 days at room temperature. Bread freezes well for up to 2 months.

You can substitute full-fat plain yogurt for the sour cream.

SPEEDY BAGELS

MAKES 8 BAGELS · ·

These bagels don't involve yeast or boiling in water; they go right from bowl to oven. They have a wonderful chewy texture that the family will enjoy on any occasion.

3 cups (750 mL) all-purpose flour

2 tsp (10 mL) baking powder

1 tsp (5 mL) baking soda

1 tsp (5 mL) garlic powder

1 tsp (5 mL) dried Italian seasoning

½ tsp (2 mL) salt

2 cups (500 mL) plain Greek (2%) yogurt

1 Preheat oven to 400°F (200°C). Line a baking sheet with parchment paper and set aside.

2 In a large bowl, stir together flour, baking powder, baking soda, garlic powder, Italian seasoning and salt. Add yogurt and stir until ragged dough forms. Bring dough together using your hands in bowl. Dump onto floured work surface and knead until smooth dough forms and is not sticky; sprinkle with additional flour as necessary.

3 Divide dough into 8 pieces and roll each into a 9-inch (23 cm) rope. Pinch edges together to form a circle and place on prepared pan. Bake for about 15 minutes or until golden. Let cool slightly.

VARIATIONS

EVERYTHING BAGEL VARIATION: Omit Italian seasoning and garlic powder and substitute 2 tsp (10 mL) everything bagel seasoning.

CHEDDAR VARIATION: Add ½ cup (125 mL) shredded sharp (old) Cheddar cheese with yogurt and sprinkle tops with ½ cup (125 mL) more Cheddar before baking.

CINNAMON RAISIN VARIATION: Omit garlic powder and Italian seasoning and substitute 2 tsp (10 mL) ground cinnamon. Stir in ¾ cup (175 mL) raisins with yogurt.

TIPS

Place bagels in a freezer bag or airtight container for up to 1 month. Thaw at room temperature before enjoying warmed or toasted.

Want a smaller bagel? Divide dough into 12 and reduce baking time slightly.

VEGETABLE HERB SPREAD

MAKES ABOUT 1½ CUPS (375 ML) · · ·

This spread is delicious for the Speedy Bagels on page 28, but you may enjoy it as a spread for any sandwich! It's a colorful and creamy way to add more veggies to your day.

8 oz (250 g) brick-style cream cheese, softened

1 small carrot, shredded

¼ cup (60 mL) finely diced red bell pepper

1 tbsp (15 mL) chopped fresh dill

1 tbsp (15 mL) chopped fresh parsley

1 small garlic clove, minced

¼ tsp (1 mL) salt

Pinch black pepper

1 In a large bowl, using an electric mixer, beat cream cheese until smooth. Beat in carrot, pepper, dill, parsley, garlic, salt and pepper until well combined.

2 Cover and refrigerate for up to 1 week.

VARIATION

CHEDDAR VARIATION: Add ½ cup (125 mL) shredded sharp (old) Cheddar with veggies.

*I made a vegetable joke.
But no one carrot all.*

RASPBERRY MAPLE BUTTER

MAKES 1 CUP (250 ML) · · · ·

We love the gorgeous pink color of this fruity spread.
Enjoy this burst of flavor on scones, croissants, bagels,
french toast, pancakes and muffins.

½ cup (125 mL) butter, softened

¼ cup (60 mL) fresh raspberries

3 tbsp (45 mL) raspberry jam

1 tbsp (15 mL) maple syrup

1 In a bowl, add butter, raspberries, jam and maple syrup. Using a fork, mash until well combined and a few chunks of raspberry remain. If you prefer a smoother texture, combine ingredients in a food processor and process until smooth.

2 Transfer to an air-tight container and refrigerate until ready to use. Store any leftovers in the refrigerator for up to 4 days.

TIP
Divide butter into smaller portions and freeze for up to 2 months.

It happened before my berry eyes.

BLUEBERRY BRUNCH SANGRIA

SERVES 8 · · ·

Your next get together should include a unique drink like this. The frozen blueberries help keep it cold while the tender fresh blueberries are easy to bite into. Emily's friend Juliet enjoyed this sangria and notes that adding tequila makes a fabulous twist!

3 cups (750 mL) blueberry juice

3 cups (750 mL) limeade or lemonade

2 cups (500 mL) orange juice

1 tsp (5 mL) grated lime zest

2 tbsp (30 mL) lime juice

3/4 cup (175 mL) white wine or tequila (optional)

2 cups (500 mL) frozen blueberries

1 cup (250 mL) fresh blueberries

4 sprigs fresh mint

Ice cubes

Lime slices (optional)

1 In a large pitcher, combine blueberry juice, limeade, orange juice, lime zest and juice, and wine, if using. Stir in frozen and fresh blueberries and mint sprigs. Chill until ready to serve.

2 Add ice cubes to pitcher along with lime slices, if using, when ready to serve.

FROZEN PEACH BELLINI COCKTAILS

SERVES 8 ·  ·

It's time to clink your glasses with this fruity drink! Enjoy as a refreshing slushie to sip on during brunch and other get togethers. Grenadine is a deep red colored syrup made from pomegranate juice that creates a beautiful pink ombre effect in the glass.

4 cups (1 L) frozen peaches

1½ cups (375 mL) peach nectar or apricot juice

1 lime, juiced

Grenadine syrup

3 cups (750 mL) chilled sparkling wine or champagne

Fresh peaches to garnish (optional)

1 In a blender, add frozen peaches, peach nectar and lime juice, blend until smooth. In each glass, add about 1 tsp (5 mL) of grenadine, then add about ½ cup (125 mL) of peach purée. Top up each glass with sparkling wine. Garnish with fresh peach slices, if desired.

TIP
For a non-alcoholic version, substitute the wine with sparkling water, club soda or lemon-lime soda.

APPETIZERS

DILL PICKLE DIP

MAKES 2 CUPS (500 ML) · · ·

This dip is so tasty, you might want to double the recipe.
Our homemade version of the popular dill pickle dip takes
only minutes to prepare and it's bursting with flavor and
perfect for any party, backyard get-together and game time.
Serve with raw vegetables, potato chips and crackers.

- 8 oz (250 g) brick-style cream cheese, softened
- 1/4 cup (60 mL) plain (2%) Greek yogurt or sour cream
- 1/4 cup (60 mL) mayonnaise
- 1/2 cup (125 mL) finely chopped dill pickles
- 1/4 cup (60 mL) chopped fresh dill
- 1/4 (60 mL) chopped green onion
- 2 tbsp (30 mL) dill pickle juice
- 1/2 tsp (2 mL) black pepper
- 1/2 tsp (2 mL) garlic powder
- Chopped dill pickles for garnish

1. In a medium bowl, combine cream cheese, yogurt and mayonnaise and mix until smooth. Stir in dill pickles, dill, green onion, pickle juice, pepper and garlic powder until combined. Garnish with extra dill pickle if desired.

2. Cover and refrigerate at least 1 hour before serving.

MAKE AHEAD

If you want to make this a day ahead, omit the pickle juice, as the chopped pickles will continue to release their juice. Check the consistency of the dip before serving; if you prefer it to be a little thinner, then add more pickle juice, a little at a time.

What do you get when you cross a pickle with an alligator? You get a crocodill.

FRENCH ONION DIP

MAKES 2 CUPS (500 ML) · · ·

Rich and creamy French onion dip is a party favorite — set it out and it disappears fast! Adding water during cooking not only aids in cooking the onions, it also helps prevent them from burning in the pan. This delicious dip multitasks as a condiment; spread it in a hamburger or sandwich or spoon onto roasted potatoes.

1 tbsp (15 mL) butter

1 tbsp (15 mL) canola oil

2 large onions, finely diced

3/4 cup (175 mL) sour cream or full fat plain yogurt

3/4 cup (175 mL) mayonnaise

2 tsp (10 mL) lemon juice

1 tsp (5 mL) packed brown sugar

1 tsp (5 mL) Worcestershire sauce

1/2 tsp (2 mL) dried thyme

1/4 tsp (1 mL) garlic powder

Salt and black pepper to taste

1 In a heavy skillet over medium-high heat, melt butter with oil. Add onions and cook for 5 minutes; add a few spoons of water and continue cooking and scraping the bottom browned bits for about 15 minutes. Adding more water as needed, cook until onions are soft and have turned a deep golden brown color. Remove from heat and cool a few minutes.

2 Meanwhile, in a medium bowl, combine sour cream, mayonnaise, lemon juice, brown sugar, Worcestershire, thyme and garlic powder.

3 Stir in cooled onions; season to taste with salt and pepper. Serve with crackers, bagels, sliced baguette or potato chips.

TIP
Store in an airtight container and refrigerate for up to 3 days.

LOADED WHITE BEAN HUMMUS

SERVES 6 TO 8 · · · ·

This bean dip is made in a blender to create a super smooth and creamy consistency. Fresh toppings add gorgeous color, and the Middle Eastern herb-and-spice blend, za'atar, adds a wonderful tangy, earthy flavor. Serve with toasted flatbread, crackers, tortilla chips or your favorite raw vegetables.

BEAN DIP

1 can (19 oz/540 mL) white beans (cannellini, great Northern, navy), rinsed and drained

2 tbsp (30 mL) tahini

2 tbsp (30 mL) extra virgin olive oil

2 tbsp (30 mL) lemon juice

1/2 tsp (2 mL) grated lemon zest

2 garlic cloves, minced

1/2 tsp (2 mL) hot pepper flakes

1 tbsp (15 mL) water

Salt and black pepper, to taste

TOPPINGS

1/2 English cucumber, finely diced

1 cup (250 mL) grape tomatoes, halved

1/2 cup (125 mL) crumbled feta cheese

1/3 cup (75 mL) chopped fresh parsley

3 tbsp (45 mL) finely diced red onion

1 tbsp (15 mL) za'atar spice mix

1 In a blender, add beans, tahini, oil, lemon juice, lemon zest, garlic and pepper flakes; blend until combined. Mixture will be coarse. Add water and blend until mixture is very smooth. Add more water if mixture is too thick. Blend in salt and pepper to taste.

2 Transfer to a serving platter and sprinkle with toppings.

MAKE AHEAD

The toppings can be chopped and refrigerated overnight.

The bean dip on its own can be made ahead. Cover and refrigerate for up to 3 days.

TIPS

This can also be made in a food processor, however, the texture may be slightly grainy, but still just as delicious.

You can find za'atar spice in the spice or international section of the grocery store.

Za'atar brands vary in their flavor, so feel free to add more according to your taste.

SEVEN-LAYER DIP

SERVES 12 ·  ·

Emily's cousin Phyllis is known for making a version of this dip for literally every birthday party, work potluck and, yes, even the Super Bowl party! You will love this version with a few Best of Bridge twists.

1 can (14 oz/398 mL) refried beans

1 container (7.5 oz/227 g) roasted red pepper dip or hummus

8 oz (250 g) brick-style cream cheese, softened

1³/₄ cups (425 mL) plain Greek yogurt

1 tsp (5 mL) garlic powder

1 tsp (5 mL) smoked paprika

2 avocados, diced

2 tbsp (30 mL) lime juice

¹/₄ tsp (1 mL) salt

1¹/₂ cups (375 mL) medium chunky salsa

3 cups (750 mL) shredded romaine or iceberg lettuce

3 cups (750 mL) shredded sharp (old) Cheddar cheese

¹/₂ cup (125 mL) chopped roasted red pepper or black olives

2 small jalapeño peppers or 1 large jalapeño, seeded and thinly sliced

1 Lightly spray a 13- by 9-inch (33 by 23 cm) casserole dish with nonstick cooking spray.

2 In a bowl, stir together refried beans and dip. Spread onto bottom of prepared dish.

3 In another bowl, using an electric hand mixer, beat cream cheese, yogurt, garlic powder and smoked paprika until smooth. Spread over top of hummus layer.

4 Toss avocado with lime juice and salt. Sprinkle over top of cream cheese layer. Spoon salsa all over. Sprinkle with lettuce, then cheese over top. Sprinkle with roasted red pepper and jalapeño peppers all over. Cover with plastic wrap and refrigerate for at least 1 hour or up to 2 days.

5 Serve with thick tortilla chips or potato chips, or with a spoon and enjoy on baked potatoes or a bun. We are not kidding — you will love it!

TIPS

Need one for today and another for tomorrow? No problem, divide the ingredients among two 9- or 10-inch (23 or 25 cm) deep-dish pie plates!

You can change up the layers by reversing the orders a little too. Try putting the cream cheese layer on the bottom and then the refried bean layer to enjoy a whole new taste sensation in your mouth!

PUFF PASTRY-WRAPPED BRIE WITH MAPLE WALNUT FILLING

SERVES 12 · · ·

Rich creamy Brie plus the sweet addition of raisins
and maple syrup makes an appetizer that is fit for
any large gathering. The golden crust of puff pastry
means this is a favorite for entertaining.

½ cup (125 mL) chopped walnuts, toasted

½ cup (125 mL) golden raisins

¼ cup (60 mL) pure maple syrup

1 sheet butter puff pastry, thawed

1 round (10 oz/300 g) Brie cheese

1 In a bowl, stir together walnuts, raisins and maple syrup until combined well; set aside.

2 Preheat oven to 400°F (200°C). Line a baking sheet with parchment paper.

3 On lightly floured work surface, roll out puff pastry to about a 12-inch (30 cm) circle.

4 Using a large serrated knife, cut Brie round in half crosswise to make two circles. Separate pieces and spoon walnut mixture onto one half of the Brie. Top with remaining Brie half. Place Brie in center of pastry and fold pastry over top overlapping each piece decoratively to cover Brie.

5 Place on prepared sheet and bake for about 20 minutes or until pastry is golden brown. Let cool for about 10 minutes before serving.

TIPS

Wrap prepared Brie with plastic wrap and refrigerate for up to 2 hours before baking.

Instead of store-bought pastry, you can also use a ½ recipe of our Easy Puff Pastry on page 54.

CRANBERRY ROSEMARY NUT BRIE

SERVES 6 TO 8 · · ·

This tasty topping combines sweet, tart and savory.
Bake and serve the topped cheese round until it is soft
and warm in a special Brie baker if you have one.

1 round (7 to 10 oz/200 to 300 g) Brie cheese

1/3 cup (75 mL) dried cranberries

2 tbsp (30 mL) orange liqueur or juice

2 tbsp (30 mL) chopped walnuts, toasted

1 tbsp (15 mL) chopped fresh parsley

1/2 tsp (2 mL) dried rosemary

1 small garlic clove, minced

1 Preheat oven to 400°F (200°C). Line a small baking dish with parchment paper. Place Brie in prepared dish.

2 Place cranberries in a microwaveable bowl and add liqueur. Cover with plastic wrap and microwave on High for 45 seconds or until fragrant and cranberries are softened. Stir in nuts, parsley, rosemary and garlic. Spoon onto cheese and bake for 10 to 15 minutes or until side of Brie feels soft.

TIPS

Make the cranberry rosemary mixture and serve on its own alongside your favorite roast turkey, pork or chicken.

If the Brie needs a hint of sweetness, you can add a drizzle of honey or maple syrup. Be sure to taste-test it first to see what you think.

RASPBERRY CHIPOTLE-TOPPED BRIE

SERVES 6 TO 8 · · ·

Sweet and spicy makes a perfect match to any rich creamy cheese. Thaw and drain the frozen raspberries for best results.

1 round (7 to 10 oz/200 to 300 g) Brie cheese

1 cup (250 mL) frozen raspberries, thawed and drained

1 tbsp (15 mL) granulated sugar

3 tbsp (45 mL) chopped pecans, toasted

1 tbsp (15 mL) chopped fresh parsley

1 small canned chipotle pepper, minced

1 Preheat oven to 400°F (200°C). Line a small baking dish with parchment paper. Place Brie in prepared dish.

2 In a bowl and using a fork, crush raspberries with sugar. Stir in pecans, parsley and chipotle. Spoon onto Brie and bake for 10 to 15 minutes or until side of Brie feels soft.

THYME AND OLIVE-MARINATED GOAT CHEESE

SERVES 6 · · ·

This combination is a favorite of Emily's and she serves it at almost every gathering at her home — even the kids love this! People can dig into it and enjoy as much as they like, or you can serve it on crostini with an extra drizzle of olive oil.

1 log (10 oz/300 g) goat cheese

¼ cup (60 mL) chopped pitted black sun-dried olives

3 garlic cloves, minced

2 tsp (10 mL) chopped fresh thyme

¼ tsp (1 mL) freshly ground black pepper

Extra virgin olive oil

Aged balsamic vinegar

1 Using dental floss, cut goat cheese into thin medallions. Place in a small casserole dish, overlapping slightly if necessary.

2 Sprinkle cheese with olives, garlic, thyme and pepper. Drizzle with enough oil to coat cheese. Drizzle vinegar over top; cover and refrigerate for at least 2 hours for flavors to develop.

TIPS

Serve with crostini or crackers. It is just as delicious on warm baguette slices.

MAKE YOUR OWN CROSTINI: Slice a baguette and place slices on a baking sheet. Brush slices with extra virgin olive oil and toast in 400°F (200°C) oven for about 8 minutes or until light golden. Sprinkle with salt.

ANTIPASTO PLATTER

SERVES 4 TO 6

When you visit an Italian deli or grocery store, you will notice a vast array of ingredients that are perfect for an antipasto platter. Use different cutting boards or serving platters to showcase the variety available to your guests and pair ingredients that you like the flavor of together.

8 oz (250 g) thinly sliced prosciutto

4 oz (125 g) thinly sliced hot or mild salami

4 oz (125 g) thinly sliced sopressata or capiccollo (hot or mild)

1 cup (250 mL) black or green olives (or a mixture)

2 cups (500 mL) grape tomatoes

1 cup (250 mL) sliced roasted red peppers, drained

1 small wedge of Parmesan or extra-sharp (extra-old) Cheddar cheese

1 cup (250 mL) ricotta cheese

Liquid chestnut or buckwheat honey (optional)

Fresh ground black pepper

1 cup (250 mL) pickled vegetables (such as carrots, cauliflower and celery)

Fresh herbs, dried figs or dates, seedless grapes and nuts (optional)

1 Loosely place prosciutto slices on serving board. Roll salami and place on another spot on the board. Fan out the sopressata on the board in another spot. Place the olives in a small bowl and fit them into an empty spot on the board. Pile the roasted peppers on another empty spot on the board. Tuck in the Parmesan on the board and break some of the cheese up into little nuggets with a cheese knife or fork right on the board.

2 Place the ricotta cheese on a small plate that will fit on the board and drizzle it with honey, if using, and sprinkle with pepper. Add the pickled vegetables all around or in a little bowl on the board.

3 Garnish the board with fresh herbs, figs, grapes and nuts if desired.

VARIATIONS

VEGAN ANTIPASTO: Omit the sliced meats and cheeses and substitute with vegan cheeses and spreads, and include the roasted red peppers, pickled vegetables and olives. They will add a wonderful color and texture difference to the board.

FRUIT BOARD: Slice half a cantaloupe and honeydew melons into thin slices and add large strawberries and small bunches of grapes. Try adding some starfruit slices or chunks of dragonfruit.

CANDY BOARD: Pick up 6 of your favorite kinds of candy from the bulk store. We like sour candy, chocolate, chocolate-coated nuts or raisins, lollipops, sticky candy and toffee. Display on a board with tongs for everyone to help themselves.

PARMESAN BUTTER POPCORN

MAKES ABOUT 8 CUPS (2 L) · · ·

For awards shows, or any night where celebrities dress in designer names and bask in the luxury of all things expensive, you can do the same, using some of the finest ingredients to create buttery rich popcorn as good as this.

2 tbsp (30 mL) canola oil

1/2 cup (125 mL) popcorn kernels

1/2 cup (125 mL) butter

1/4 cup (60 mL) freshly grated Parmesan cheese

Pinch each kosher salt and freshly ground black pepper

1 In a large pot, heat oil over medium heat. Add kernels and shake pot to coat kernels. Cover with lid and cook, swirling pot occasionally until popping begins.

2 Loosen lid and set slightly askew to create a small steam vent; cook, swirling pot for about 4 minutes or until popping begins to slow down. Remove from heat and let stand covered until all popping stops. Remove lid and place in large bowl.

3 In a small saucepan, melt butter over medium heat. Place cheese in small bowl. Gently pour butter into cheese, making sure to pour in only the butter and not the creamy whey. Discard whey. Add salt and pepper to butter and cheese mixture and stir until cheese is melted.

4 Drizzle over popcorn and toss gently until popcorn is well coated.

TIPS

Have an automatic corn popper? Omit oil and follow manufacturer's instructions to make popcorn and drizzle with butter and cheese mixture.

For microwave popcorn, omit oil and use one large bag of plain popcorn and drizzle with butter and cheese mixture.

You will need 8 cups (2 L) of popped popcorn for this Parmesan butter coating. If you end up with less popcorn, you can drizzle with less of the topping.

Not using the whey helps keep the popcorn crispy.

GREEN PEA PESTO CROSTINI

MAKES 20 PIECES · · ·

Crispy crostini topped with this brilliant creamy green dip makes a delicious contrast in texture. Top with a generous sprinkle of smoked paprika and Parmesan cheese to elevate a simple appetizer to something special. Both the spread and crostini can be made ahead of time so you can relax with your family and guests.

GREEN PEA PESTO

3 cups (750 mL) frozen green peas, partially thawed

⅓ cup (75 mL) basil pesto

¼ cup (60 mL) ricotta cheese

2 tbsp (30 mL) olive oil

1 tsp (5 mL) lemon juice

½ tsp (2 mL) each salt and black pepper

CROSTINI

1 baguette, sliced into about 20 pieces

¼ cup (60 mL) extra virgin olive oil

½ tsp (2 mL) each salt and black pepper

Smoked paprika or hot pepper flakes

Grated Parmesan cheese

1 GREEN PEA PESTO: In a bowl of a food processor, add peas, pesto, ricotta, olive oil, lemon juice, salt and pepper. Pulse to desired consistency. Makes about 2 cups (500 mL).

2 CROSTINI: Preheat oven to 400°F (200°C). Brush baguette slices on both sides with oil. Place on a large rimmed baking sheet in a single layer. Bake for 8 minutes or until they are light and golden, but still a bit soft in the center. Sprinkle with salt and pepper.

3 To serve, spread green pea pesto onto crostini. Garnish each with a good sprinkle of smoked paprika and Parmesan on top.

MAKE AHEAD

You can make the crostini up to 1 day ahead. Recrisp in 350°F (180°C) oven for a few minutes before using, if desired.

TIPS

Refrigerate green pea pesto spread for up to 3 days. It can be frozen for up to 1 month. Store in a freezer-safe container. Alternatively, portion in an ice cube tray, and once frozen, transfer to a freezer-safe container.

For larger crostini, cut bread on a diagonal. For smaller crostini, cut perpendicular to the baguette.

HERBED CHEESE AND ZUCCHINI TART

SERVES 12 ·

We love an appetizer with a big flavor impact that uses just a few ingredients. This recipe makes two tarts, can be assembled ahead of time, stored in the refrigerator, then popped in the oven when you're ready to bake. Any leftovers are delicious served on the side with your favorite soup. Simply reheat in the oven on a rack to ensure the bottom crisps up.

1 recipe Easy Puff Pastry (see page 54)

1 package (5 oz/150 g) Boursin Garlic and Fine Herbs cheese

1 medium zucchini (about 10 oz/300 g), thinly sliced into rounds

2 tsp (10 mL) extra virgin olive oil

Pinch each of salt and black pepper

1 large egg, lightly beaten

1 Preheat oven to 375°F (190°C). On a large piece of parchment paper, sprinkle a little flour. Using a lightly floured rolling pin, roll out one piece of the pastry to make a 10- by 8-inch (25 by 20 cm) rectangle; leaving on parchment, transfer to a baking sheet. Using the tip of a knife, score a 1/2-inch (1 cm) border around the edge. Brush edges with egg wash.

2 Spread half of the cheese evenly over the pastry, within the border. Lay half of the zucchini slices on top, so they are slightly overlapping each other. Brush zucchini with 1 tsp (5 mL) oil; sprinkle with a little salt and pepper. Repeat with remaining pastry and toppings.

3 Bake for 45 to 50 minutes, until pastry is golden brown. Let cool 5 minutes before cutting into pieces.

MAKE AHEAD

Can be prepared 2 hours ahead; brush with egg wash just before baking. Store in refrigerator until ready to bake.

TIP

No time to make pastry from scratch? You can also use a store-bought 1 lb (450 to 500 g) package of puff pastry.

EASY PUFF PASTRY

MAKES ABOUT 1 LB (500 G) · · ·

Try this easy shortcut version of homemade puff pastry with buttery, flaky results. The key to success is in the multiple folding of the dough. Try this pastry with our Herbed Zucchini Cheese Tart on page 52, our Puff Pastry-Wrapped Brie with Maple Walnut Filling on page 43 and our Aussie Beef pie recipe on page 116.

1/3 cup (75 mL) cold water

2 tsp (10 mL) vinegar

1 2/3 cups (400 mL) all-purpose flour

1/2 tsp (2 mL) salt

1 cup (250 mL) cold butter, chopped

1   In a measuring cup, combine water and vinegar; set aside.

2   In the bowl of a food processor, add flour and salt; pulse to combine. Add the butter and pulse about six times, until butter is about the size of large peas. Remove lid and pour water and vinegar evenly over mixture. Pulse three or four times until a loose, ragged dough forms. (Do not let form into ball.)

3   Turn mixture out onto a lightly floured surface and gently press it together with a few quick kneads. Lightly flour a rolling pin and roll into a 12- by 8-inch (30 by 20 cm) rectangle; starting at short end, fold dough over into thirds like a letter. Turn the dough 90 degrees. Repeat rolling, folding and rotating three more times, using flour sparingly. Fold back into thirds and divide dough in two; wrap each piece tightly in plastic and refrigerate 1 hour or until ready to use.

MAKE AHEAD
Wrap well and refrigerate for up to 3 days or freeze in airtight container for up to 2 months. If frozen, thaw in the refrigerator overnight.

NOORBANU'S VEGETABLE PAKORAS

MAKES ABOUT 40 · ·

These delicious crispy fritters are a great party food. Sylvia's friend Karen shares her recipe, which she learned from her Indian cooking mentor and beloved friend, the late Noorbanu Nimji. The Nimjis, originally from East Africa but with roots in Gujarat, India, call these fried snacks bhaji.

2 cups (500 mL) chickpea (chana or besan) flour

³/₄ cup (175 mL) water

1 tbsp (15 mL) finely chopped fresh cilantro

1 garlic clove, minced

1 tsp (5 mL) grated fresh ginger

1 tsp (5 mL) Sambal Oelek or Sriracha

1 tsp (5 mL) ground cumin

1 tsp (5 mL) each salt and black pepper

¹/₄ tsp (1 mL) ground turmeric

1¹/₂ cups (375 mL) grated zucchini

1 onion, halved and thinly sliced

1 medium potato, quartered and thinly sliced

5 whole jalapeño peppers, with a slit cut in their sides

³/₄ tsp (3 mL) baking powder

Canola oil for deep frying

1 In a medium bowl, sift the flour to remove any lumps. Add water and whisk until thick like pancake batter. Stir in cilantro, garlic, ginger, Sambal Oelek, cumin, salt, pepper and turmeric; let rest for 5 minutes.

2 Gently squeeze any excess moisture from zucchini, then stir into batter along with onion, potato and whole chilies. The batter should resemble thick cake batter; add a few drops of water if batter is too thick. Stir in baking powder just before frying.

3 In a large, deep, heavy pot (or a deep fryer), heat about 4 inches (10 cm) oil over medium-high heat to 350°F (180°C). Add 1 tbsp (15 mL) of the hot oil to the batter; gently mix until combined. Working in batches, carefully drop the dough by the tablespoonful into oil. Fry about 8 at a time, cooking for 1 to 2 minutes per side, or until golden brown. Using a slotted spoon or tongs, transfer pakoras to a tray lined with paper towels. Serve with chutney.

TIPS

Use both the tender stems and the leaves of cilantro.

If you don't have a thermometer, you can judge if the oil is ready by dropping a bit of batter in. If it sizzles, it's ready.

These are delicious served with lemon wedges, hot sauce and coriander, or Indian-style tomato or tamarind chutneys.

CHICKPEA FRIES WITH DIPS

SERVES 8 ·

Crispy on the outside and creamy on the inside, these fries are a delicious snack that we've paired with a choice of flavored dips. These fries are popular in France and are known as panisse. Chickpea flour, sometimes labelled as garbanzo bean or chana flour, can be found in the baking section, health food section or the international aisle of the grocery store.

4 cups (1 L) water

2 tbsp (30 mL) olive oil

2½ tsp (12 mL) salt

1 tsp (5 mL) garlic powder

1½ tsp (7 mL) ground cumin

½ tsp (2 mL) black pepper

2 cups (500 mL) chickpea flour

Canola oil for frying

1 Lightly oil a 13- by 9-inch (33 by 23 cm) baking pan; set aside.

2 In a medium pot over medium-high heat, bring water, olive oil, salt, garlic powder, cumin and pepper to a boil. Reduce heat to medium and whisk in chickpea flour, whisking constantly until thick and smooth, about 2 to 3 minutes. Scrape into prepared pan and smooth top; let cool. After 30 minutes, turn the firm mixture out onto a cutting board and cut into sticks, about 3 by ½ inch (7.5 by 1 cm).

3 In a deep heavy skillet over medium-high heat, heat ½ inch (1 cm) oil. Line a baking tray with paper towel; set aside. Working in batches, carefully add chickpea fries and cook until golden and crispy on all sides, about 6 minutes. Transfer to prepared baking tray. Repeat with remaining fries, adding more oil as needed.

4 Serve warm with a choice of flavored mayonnaise.

MAKE AHEAD

Chickpea mixture can be made 1 day ahead; cover and store in refrigerator.

FLAVORED MAYONNAISE FOUR WAYS

Combine any one of the following with ½ cup (125 mL) mayonnaise to make a flavored dip for the chickpea fries: 2 tbsp (30 mL) basil pesto, or 1 tbsp (15 mL) za'atar spice mix, or 2 tsp (10 mL) Sriracha or harissa paste.

SOUPS AND SANDWICHES

~

ZUCCHINI SOUP

SERVES 6 ·

A delicious silky soup that can be enjoyed hot or cold,
it's perfect to make when zucchini season is in full
force and you're looking for tasty ways to use it up!

2 tbsp (30 mL) canola oil

1 onion, chopped

2 lb (1 kg) zucchini, chopped

2 celery stalks, chopped

2/3 cup (150 mL) lightly packed fresh parsley, chopped

1 garlic clove, minced

1 1/2 tsp (7 mL) dried thyme

3 cups (750 mL) ready-to-use vegetable or chicken broth

1/2 cup (125 mL) heavy or whipping (35%) cream or full-fat coconut milk

2 tsp (10 mL) lemon juice

Salt and black pepper, to taste

Finely chopped fresh parsley, optional, for garnish

1 In a large pot, heat oil over medium-high heat; add onion and sauté for 3 minutes, stirring occasionally, until onions begin to soften and brown. Add zucchini, celery, parsley, garlic and thyme; sauté for 1 minute. Add broth and bring to a boil, then reduce heat to medium. Cover and let simmer for 15 to 20 minutes, until vegetables are tender.

2 Remove from heat, stir in cream, let cool slightly and transfer in batches into a blender. Blend soup until smooth, then return soup to pot.

3 Stir in lemon juice; season to taste with salt and pepper. Ladle into bowls and garnish with chopped parsley if desired.

MAKE AHEAD

Soup can be prepared up to 2 days ahead. Cover and refrigerate.

CARROT COCONUT GINGER SOUP

SERVES 6 TO 8 · · ·

Enjoy this cozy golden soup for when the temperature drops outside — it will fill your house with delicious aromas. The coconut milk adds a creamy satisfying richness to each bowl. If you give the carrots a good scrub to remove any dirt, you can skip the peeling.

2 tbsp (30 mL) canola oil

1 large onion, chopped

2 lbs (1 kg) carrots, chopped

4 garlic cloves, minced

2 tbsp (30 mL) grated fresh ginger

1 tsp (5 mL) curry powder

1 tsp (5 mL) ground cumin

4 cups (1 L) ready-to-use vegetable broth

1 tbsp (15 mL) packed brown sugar

1 tsp (5 mL) soy sauce

1/2 cup (125 mL) coconut milk

Salt and black pepper, to taste

1/2 cup (125 mL) chopped fresh cilantro

1 In a large pot, heat oil over medium-high heat. Add onion and sauté for 10 minutes, stirring occasionally, until onions begin to soften. Add carrots, garlic, ginger, curry powder and cumin, and sauté for 30 seconds.

2 Add broth, brown sugar and soy sauce, bring to a boil, then reduce heat to medium. Cover and let simmer for 25 minutes, or until carrots are tender.

3 Let soup cool a few minutes, then transfer to a blender. Purée the soup in batches. Return soup to pot; over medium heat, reheat soup and stir in coconut milk; season to taste with salt and pepper.

4 Ladle into bowls and garnish with cilantro.

MAKE AHEAD

Refrigerate the soup for up to 4 days or freeze for up to 3 months.

TIPS

You can also use an immersion blender to purée the soup until smooth.

Store any leftover canned coconut milk in the fridge for up to 7 days. Coconut milk also freezes well. Use remaining coconut milk to stir into smoothies, hot oatmeal or our recipe for Zucchini Soup, page 60.

SPINACH AND PEA SOUP

SERVES 5 ·

Soup brings so much comfort around the table.
This veggie-friendly soup includes a potato to add a velvety texture without cream. It's quick and easy enough to make a double batch to share with friends and family to show that you care. Serve with your favorite bread or topped with croutons.

2 tbsp (30 mL) canola oil

1 onion, chopped

1 medium potato, peeled and grated

2 tsp (10 mL) dried Italian seasoning

1 garlic clove, minced

6 cups (1.5 L) ready-to-use vegetable or chicken broth

10 oz (300 g) baby spinach (about 8 cups/2 L)

2 cups (500 mL) frozen peas, thawed

1/3 cup (75 mL) chopped fresh parsley

1 tsp (5 mL) lemon juice

Salt and black pepper, to taste

Parmesan cheese or nutritional yeast flakes for garnish

1 In a large pot, heat oil over medium-high heat, add onion and potato; sauté for 5 minutes, until onion begins to soften and potato is tender. Add Italian seasoning and garlic, sauté for 20 seconds, then add broth. Cover and bring to a boil, reduce heat to medium and cook 6 minutes. Add spinach, peas and parsley, cover and cook 5 minutes.

2 Remove from heat, stir in lemon juice and season to taste with salt and pepper. Using an immersion blender, blend soup to desired consistency.

3 Ladle into bowls and sprinkle with Parmesan cheese or nutritional yeast flakes.

TIPS

Refrigerate any leftovers in an air-tight container for up to 2 days. Freeze for up to 2 months.

For a very smooth velvety texture, purée soup in a blender.

This soup is perfect for using up wilted spinach.

CREAMY PAPRIKA MUSHROOM SOUP

SERVES 6 · · ·

Sylvia's family are big fans of this rich hearty soup.
The amazing taste comes from using plenty of
mushrooms and two kinds of paprika.

2 tbsp (30 mL) butter

1 1/2 lbs (750 g) assorted
fresh mushrooms, sliced

1 onion, finely chopped

2 garlic cloves, minced

2 tsp (10 mL) dried dill

2 tsp (10 mL) sweet paprika

1 tsp (5 mL) smoked
paprika

1 tsp (5 mL) salt

1 tsp (5 mL) dried thyme

4 cups (1 L) ready-to-use
vegetable or chicken
broth

3 tbsp (45 mL) water

2 tbsp (30 mL) cornstarch

1 cup (250 mL) heavy or
whipping (35%) cream
or full-fat coconut milk

2 tsp (10 mL) balsamic
vinegar

2 tbsp (30 mL) chopped
fresh parsley

1. In a large pot, over medium-high heat, add butter, mushrooms and onions, stirring occasionally for 15 minutes, until mushrooms are browned and onions are tender. Stir in garlic, dill, sweet paprika, smoked paprika, salt and thyme and cook 30 seconds.

2. Add broth and bring to a boil; reduce heat to medium-low, cover and simmer gently for 10 minutes.

3. In a small bowl, combine water and cornstarch; stir into soup along with cream. Increase heat to medium-high, bringing soup to a gentle boil; boil for one minute, stirring constantly until soup is slightly thickened. Remove from heat and stir in vinegar.

4. Ladle into bowls and top with parsley.

MAKE AHEAD

Soup can be made up to 3 days ahead; store in refrigerator.

TIP

Slice mushrooms quickly with a food processor or mandoline.

BACON SWEET POTATO SOUP

SERVES 6 TO 8 · · ·

This soup is perfect for sharing with family and friends. Emily's friend Pam brought it to a celebration of a job well done making sausages, and it was hailed as a wonderfully delicious soup by the kids at the table!

8 oz (250 g) bacon slices, chopped

2 sweet potatoes (about 1½ lb/750 g), peeled and chopped

2 potatoes (about 12 oz/375 g), peeled and chopped

1 carrot, chopped

1 onion, chopped

2 garlic cloves, chopped

1 tsp (5 mL) dried sage

1 tsp (5 mL) dried thyme

4 cups (1 L) ready- to-use vegetable or chicken broth

1 cup (250 mL) heavy or whipping (35%) cream

¼ tsp (1 mL) each salt and black pepper

1 cup (250 mL) shredded sharp (old) Cheddar cheese

1 In a large pot, cook bacon over medium-high heat until crispy. Remove with slotted spoon to paper towel lined plate. Reduce heat to medium.

2 In the same pot, stir in sweet potatoes, potatoes, carrot and onion; cook for about 5 minutes or until well coated. Stir in garlic, sage and thyme; cook for 1 minute.

3 Pour in broth and bring to a simmer. Cover and simmer for about 20 minutes or until vegetables are very soft.

4 Using an immersion blender, purée soup. Alternatively, ladle into blender or food processor in batches to purée. Stir in cream, salt and pepper and heat through. Stir in bacon and cheese. When cheese is melted, ladle soup into bowls to serve.

TIPS

Cook up extra bacon or reserve some for garnishing the soup if desired.

Need a creamier touch? Drizzle each bowl with more cream if you like.

Add a fresh zip with chopped chives on top when serving.

TOFU BANH MI

SERVES 4 ·

The toasted bun and pickled vegetables add
great texture in this Vietnamese-style sandwich.
Each bite bursts with a balance of sweet, salty, tart flavor.

TOFU

1 lb (500 g) firm or extra
firm tofu

3 tbsp (45 mL) packed
brown sugar

2 tbsp (30 mL) vegan fish
sauce

1 tbsp (15 mL) lime juice

1 tbsp (15 mL) soy sauce

1 tbsp (15 mL) canola oil

1 garlic clove, minced

PICKLED VEGGIES

1 tbsp (15 mL) cider vinegar

1 tbsp (15 mL) granulated
sugar

1 garlic clove, minced

1/2 tsp (2 mL) salt

1 carrot, cut into
matchsticks

3 red radishes, thinly sliced

SANDWICH

4 crusty mini baguettes,
lightly toasted

1/4 cup (60 mL) mayonnaise

1 tbsp (15 mL) Sriracha

1/2 English cucumber,
sliced thinly

1 green onion, sliced

Fresh cilantro sprigs

Jalapeño slices, optional

1 TOFU: Drain tofu and cut into 1/4-inch (0.5 cm) slices. Lay out on clean tea towel or paper towels and pat dry with another towel, pressing gently to remove excess moisture. In a shallow bowl, combine brown sugar, fish sauce, lime juice, soy sauce, oil and garlic. Add tofu, flipping over to fully coat. Cover and refrigerate at least 1 hour or overnight.

2 When ready to heat, adjust oven rack to 6 inches (15 cm) below the broiler element; set oven to broil. Line a baking sheet with foil and spray with nonstick cooking spray. Place tofu on baking sheet and broil 7 to 8 minutes, then flip tofu and broil another 7 minutes, or until brown and crispy around the edges

3 PICKLED VEGGIES: Meanwhile, in a medium bowl, combine vinegar, sugar, garlic and salt; stir until sugar and salt are dissolved. Add carrot and radish, stir to combine. Let stand at least 30 minutes, stirring occasionally.

4 SANDWICH: Split baguettes, but do not cut all the way through. In a small bowl, combine mayonnaise and Sriracha sauce and evenly spread on the inside of the baguettes. Divide tofu, pickles (including a little of the pickle juice), cucumber, green onion, cilantro and jalapeños (if using) into each baguette.

VARIATION
Substitute the green onion with 1/3 cup (75 mL) thinly sliced white or yellow onion.

TIP
Use both the leaves and the tender stems of the cilantro in this sandwich.

GRILLED CHICKEN CLUB SANDWICH

Sometimes you want a classic sandwich for dinner but a little twist is always welcome. This chicken club uses chicken thighs, which are so versatile and inexpensive you will wonder why you weren't using them before! Emily's friend Paola suggests serving this with oven fries for a fabulous side dish.

8 boneless skinless chicken thighs

1 tbsp (15 mL) canola oil

1 large garlic clove, minced

1 tsp (5 mL) chopped fresh rosemary

1/4 tsp (1 mL) each salt and black pepper

1/3 cup (75 mL) light mayonnaise

12 slices whole-grain bread, toasted

4 slices sharp (old) Cheddar cheese

4 lettuce leaves

8 slices cooked bacon

1 tomato, thinly sliced

1 In a shallow dish, toss thighs with oil, garlic, rosemary, salt and pepper.

2 Place on grill over medium-high heat and cook for about 12 minutes, turning once or until no longer pink inside. Remove to a plate.

3 Spread mayonnaise over 8 slices of the toast. Top each piece with a slice of cheese and 2 chicken thighs. Top with toast slices without mayonnaise. Place lettuce, tomato and bacon on top. Cover with remaining toast, mayonnaise side down.

4 Use four small skewers or toothpicks in each sandwich to hold the layers together, placing one in the center of each side of the bread. Using a serrated knife, carefully cut the sandwich into quarters from corner to corner.

TIPS

Want a more traditional sandwich? Simply eliminate the middle slice of bread in the sandwich.

You can also just cut the sandwich in half and enjoy!

BUTTER CHICKEN FRENCH BREAD PIZZA

SERVES 8 ·

For this recipe, we used supermarket French bread that is fluffy on the inside and has a soft crust. A quick pre-bake of the bread ensures a crisp base for the pizza toppings. For the butter chicken, be sure to use concentrated curry paste and not curry sauce.

3 tbsp (45 mL) butter

1 tbsp (15 mL) canola oil

1 small onion, thinly sliced lengthwise

6 boneless skinless chicken thighs, cut into $1/2$-inch (1 cm) pieces

3 tbsp (45 mL) tomato paste

2 tbsp (30 mL) curry paste

2 garlic cloves, minced

1 tsp (5 mL) Sriracha

$1/2$ tsp (2 mL) salt

1 cup (250 mL) half and half (10%) cream

1 loaf French bread (1 lb/500g), sliced in half horizontally

2 tbsp (30 mL) olive oil

3 cups (750 mL) shredded mozzarella cheese

Chopped fresh cilantro (optional)

Hot pepper flakes

1 In a large skillet, over medium heat, add butter, oil and onion; cook 5 minutes, stirring occasionally. Add chicken, tomato paste, curry paste, garlic, Sriracha and salt; cook 5 minutes, stirring occasionally. Stir in cream, bring to a boil uncovered, then reduce heat to low and simmer 15 minutes, until sauce is very thick. Set aside to cool slightly.

2 Meanwhile, adjust oven rack to the middle position; preheat oven to 425°F (220°C). Line a rimmed baking sheet with parchment paper or foil. Brush both sides of bread with olive oil, place cut side up on baking sheet and bake 3 minutes. Remove from oven and cool slightly.

3 Divide and spread the butter chicken sauce on top of each piece of bread. Evenly sprinkle each with cheese. Bake 10 to 12 minutes or until bread is golden brown and cheese is bubbling.

4 Turn oven off and turn on broil. Broil pizza for 2 to 3 minutes, until cheese browns. Remove from oven and sprinkle with cilantro. Cool slightly, then cut into wedges.

MAKE AHEAD
Butter chicken can be made up to 3 days in advance. Store in an airtight container in the refrigerator until ready to use.

TIP
To reheat, toast in a 350°F (180°C) oven until heated through.

CONCETTA'S MUFFULETTA SANDWICH

SERVES 4 TO 6

Our friend Connie created this wonderful sandwich
to take along on a picnic or enjoy on the deck
with family or friends and celebrate summer!

½ cup (125 mL) muffuletta spread

¼ cup (60 mL) chopped marinated artichokes

2 tbsp (30 mL) extra virgin olive oil, divided

¼ tsp (1 mL) dried oregano

1 loaf round sourdough or Calabrese bread (about 1 lb/500 g)

8 oz (250 g) sliced Genoa salami

4 oz (125 g) sliced mild capocollo or Black Forest ham

4 oz (125 g) sliced provolone or mozzarella cheese

4 oz (125 g) thinly sliced prosciutto or mortadella

¼ cup (60 mL) fresh grated Parmesan cheese

2 cups (500 mL) baby arugula

1 In a small bowl, combine muffuletta spread, artichokes, 1 tbsp (15 mL) of the oil and oregano; set aside.

2 Slice the bread in half horizontally and scoop out a bit of the inside of the bread. (Reserve for bread crumbs; see Tip.) Drizzle inside of bread with remaining oil and then spread muffuletta mixture all over inside of the loaf.

3 Layer half of the Genoa salami into bottom half of the bread. Top with capocollo, ham and provolone cheese. Top with prosciutto and remaining Genoa salami. Sprinkle with Parmesan and top with arugula.

4 Cover with top half of the loaf. Wrap tightly in plastic wrap and refrigerate for about 2 hours. If you have room in your refrigerator, sandwich the loaf between two large plates and place a heavy pan on top to weigh down the sandwich.

5 Cut into 4 or 6 pieces, depending on who is enjoying it with you!

TIPS

You can also warm the sandwich in the oven to serve if desired.

Place the crumbs you removed from the inside of the loaf into a food processor and pulse until fine crumbs. Place in a resealable bag or container and freeze until ready to use fresh bread crumbs.

Muffaletta is a tangy, flavorful spread made of olives, vinegar, chopped vegetables and spices.

FOCACCIA PIZZA SUPREME WITH HOT HONEY DRIZZLE

SERVES 10 TO 12 ·

Pizza is a classic favorite to serve as a snack or a meal when the gang's over for movie night or to watch the sports finals. Using a purchased focaccia for the crust means no making or rolling of dough and you can feed a hungry crowd easily. This loaded pizza served with a drizzle of hot honey combines savory and sweet together — it's delicious!

1/4 cup (60 mL) liquid honey

2 tsp (10 mL) hot sauce

1 loaf focaccia bread (about 1.25 lb/600 g)

2 tbsp (30 mL) extra virgin olive oil

1 cup (250 mL) marinara sauce

1/4 cup (60 mL) basil pesto

3 cups (750 mL) shredded fontina or mozzarella cheese

8 oz (250 g) thin-sliced pepperoni

1 1/2 cups (375 mL) cooked and crumbled Italian sausage

1 cup (250 mL) fresh cocktail-size bocconcini, halved

1/2 cup (125 mL) grated Parmesan cheese

1 In a small bowl, combine honey and hot sauce; set aside.

2 Adjust oven rack to middle position; preheat oven to 425°F (220°C). Set aside a parchment or foil lined baking sheet. Slice focaccia in half horizontally and brush cut sides of bread with olive oil; place cut side up on baking sheet and bake 4 minutes. Remove from oven and cool slightly.

3 Evenly spread each focaccia half with marinara sauce and pesto, then sprinkle with fontina cheese. Top with pepperoni, sausage, bocconcini and Parmesan cheese. Bake for 25 minutes. Turn oven to broil and broil pizza for 2 to 3 minutes, until cheese is golden brown.

4 Serve pizza drizzled with hot honey.

TIPS

A focaccia that is 10 by 8 inches (25 by 20 cm) works well in this recipe.

The honey is also delicious drizzled over biscuits, fried chicken or cheese. Store any leftover hot honey in a sealed container in the refrigerator for up to 1 month.

For added heat, serve with hot pepper flakes.

A French loaf or Calabrese loaf sliced in half lengthwise can substitute for the focaccia.

SALADS

~

GARDEN SALAD WITH CARROT GINGER DRESSING

SERVES 4 · ·

Garden salad doesn't have to be ho-hum. This one is inspired by the salads we've enjoyed in Japanese restaurants. The made-from-scratch dressing is full of amazing flavor — it's sweet, zesty and refreshing.

DRESSING

1 small carrot, chopped

2 tbsp (30 mL) diced onion

2 tbsp (30 mL) canola oil

2 tbsp (30 mL) cider vinegar

2 tsp (10 mL) maple syrup

2 tsp (10 mL) white miso

1 tsp (5 mL) soy sauce

1/2 tsp (2 mL) sesame oil

1/2 inch (1 cm) fresh ginger, peeled and chopped

1 garlic clove, minced

SALAD

4 cups (1 L) torn lettuce leaves

1 carrot, grated

1/2 English cucumber, sliced

1 cup (250 mL) grape tomatoes, sliced in half

1 green onion, thinly sliced

1 DRESSING: In a mini chopper or blender, add carrot, onion, oil, vinegar, maple syrup, miso, soy sauce, sesame oil, ginger and garlic; blend until smooth. Cover and store in the refrigerator until ready to use.

2 SALAD: In a large bowl, combine lettuce, carrot, cucumber, tomatoes and green onion. Drizzle with dressing to taste just before serving.

TIPS

To store dressing, pour into an airtight container and refrigerate for up to 5 days. Makes about 1/2 cup (125 mL).

White miso is mild in flavor and is also called shiro miso or sweet miso.

ROASTED VEGGIE SALAD WITH AVOCADO DRESSING

SERVES 6 TO 8 · · ·

Roasting the vegetables brings out their natural sweetness and flavor. This salad is a great way to use up of those tired-looking vegetables from the fridge. It all tastes delicious when drizzled with a creamy avocado dressing.

ROASTED VEGGIES

1 medium zucchini, cut into $\frac{1}{2}$-inch (1 cm) cubes

1 Japanese eggplant, cut into $\frac{1}{2}$-inch (1 cm) cubes

1 red bell pepper, chopped

1 small red onion, sliced

2 cups (500 mL) frozen corn kernels, thawed and drained

1 cup (250 mL) grape tomatoes

2 tbsp (30 mL) canola oil

$\frac{1}{2}$ tsp (2 mL) garlic powder

$\frac{1}{2}$ tsp (2 mL) each salt and black pepper

AVOCADO DRESSING

1 avocado, diced

$\frac{1}{4}$ cup (60 mL) sour cream

2 tbsp (30 mL) mayonnaise

2 tbsp (30 mL) lime juice

2 tbsp (30 mL) canola oil

$\frac{1}{2}$ tsp (2 mL) salt

$\frac{1}{2}$ cup (125 mL) coarsely chopped fresh basil or cilantro

1 ROASTED VEGGIES: Adjust the oven rack to 6 inches (15 cm) below the broiler element; set oven to broil. On a foil lined large rimmed baking sheet, combine salad ingredients; toss to coat evenly and spread in a single layer, spacing to avoid overcrowding.

2 Broil 15 minutes until vegetables are tender crisp, stirring halfway through roasting. Remove baking sheet from oven and set on a rack to cool for 10 minutes.

3 DRESSING: In a blender or mini food chopper, place avocado, sour cream, mayonnaise, lime juice, oil and salt. Blend until smooth. Makes 1 cup (250 mL).

4 Transfer cooled vegetables onto a serving platter. Drizzle with dressing, to taste. Sprinkle with basil or cilantro just before serving.

MAKE AHEAD

Prepare the vegetables the day before and refrigerate until ready to broil. The vegetables can also be roasted a day ahead. Cool and refrigerate until ready to serve. Bring to room temperature before drizzling with dressing.

The dressing can be made up to 2 days in advance. Store in refrigerator until ready to use.

TIP

The dressing is also delicious served as a vegetable dip, on a green salad, or drizzled over a grain bowl.

POTATO, CORN AND ASPARAGUS SALAD

SERVES 4 ·

This colorful summer in a salad is a great way
to enjoy garden and market vegetables!

4 cobs of corn, shucked

8 oz (250 g) asparagus
spears

1 red bell pepper,
quartered

3 tbsp (45 mL) canola oil,
divided

1½ lb (750 g) mini
potatoes

⅓ cup (75 mL) chopped
fresh basil

3 tbsp (45 mL) cider
vinegar

3 tbsp (45 mL) chopped
sun-dried tomatoes in oil,
drained

1 large garlic clove,
minced

2 tsp (10 mL) Dijon mustard

½ tsp (2 mL) salt

1 Toss cobs of corn, asparagus and pepper with half
of the oil. Place on greased grill over medium-high
heat; close lid and turn occasionally for about
10 minutes or until golden and crisp. When cool
enough to handle, cut corn kernels off cob and place
in a large bowl. Chop asparagus and pepper and
add to bowl.

2 Meanwhile, bring a large pot of salted water to
a boil over high heat. Add potatoes and cook
for about 10 minutes or until tender. Remove with
a slotted spoon and drain well. Quarter potatoes
and add to bowl. Stir in basil.

3 In a small bowl, whisk together remaining oil,
vinegar, sun-dried tomatoes, garlic, mustard
and salt. Toss with vegetables to coat.

TIPS

If you need to use up leftover grilled or rotisserie
chicken, be sure to add some to the salad. It will
make for a heartier salad.

Want some more zing to your salad? Emily's cousin
Maria suggests adding another splash of vinegar
when serving!

WATERMELON CUCUMBER CHERRY SALAD

SERVES 6 · · ·

This refreshing and pretty salad will be welcomed at any potluck. Each forkful is crisp, sweet, creamy and savory.

6 cups (1.5 L) cubed watermelon

1/2 English cucumber, diced

1 cup (250 mL) pitted and halved fresh cherries

1/4 small red onion, thinly sliced

1/2 cup (125 mL) crumbled feta cheese

1/4 cup (60 mL) thinly sliced fresh mint or basil leaves

2 tbsp (30 mL) lime juice

2 tbsp (30 mL) canola oil

1 tsp (5 mL) liquid honey

1/4 tsp (1 mL) each salt and black pepper

1 In a large bowl, gently combine watermelon, cucumber, cherries, onion, feta cheese and mint.

2 In a small bowl, combine lime juice, oil, honey, salt and pepper. Drizzle over salad just before serving.

TIPS

If fresh cherries are not available, substitute with fresh blueberries.

When picking a watermelon, choose one that is heavy for its size. When tapped, it should have a deep, hollow sound. Look for the creamy yellow spot; this is where the watermelon was resting on the ground and ripening on the vine.

LENTIL CITRUS SALAD

SERVES 6 TO 8 ·

Elizabeth Baird has created this salad many times over,
but this refresh includes one of her favorite ingredients,
citrus, and that makes it even more irresistible!

½ cup (125 mL) wild rice

1 cup (250 mL) green
or brown lentils

½ cup (125 mL) orzo pasta

½ cup (125 mL) currants

¼ cup (60 mL) canola oil,
divided

½ cup (125 mL) finely
chopped red onion

2 garlic cloves, minced

2 tsp (10 mL) mild curry
paste or powder

1 tsp (5 mL) ground cumin

½ tsp (2 mL) ground
turmeric

½ tsp (2 mL) salt

Pinch cayenne pepper

3 tbsp (45 mL) white
wine vinegar

1 tsp (5 mL) Dijon mustard

½ tsp (2 mL) grated
orange zest

1 large orange, peeled
and diced

½ cup (125 mL) slivered
almonds, toasted

3 tbsp (45 mL) chopped
fresh parsley

1 Bring a large pot of salted water to a boil; add wild
rice, reduce heat and simmer for 10 minutes. Add
lentils and simmer for 10 minutes; add orzo and
simmer for 5 minutes. Cook until orzo is al dente and
rice and lentils are tender but firm. Drain well and
transfer to a bowl. Add currants.

2 In a small skillet, heat 2 tbsp (30 mL) of the oil over
medium heat; cook onion and garlic for 3 minutes or
until softened. Add curry paste, cumin, turmeric, salt
and cayenne; cook, stirring, for 1 minute.

3 Remove from heat and whisk in remaining oil,
vinegar, mustard and orange zest. Pour over rice
mixture and stir well to coat. Cover and let chill in
refrigerator for at least 2 hours.

4 Add orange, almonds and parsley and stir again
to combine before serving.

TIPS

Need a gluten-free option? You can substitute
quinoa for the orzo and cook it the same length
of time.

If you are looking for a peppery addition, Emily's
friend Lisa suggests using some roughly chopped
baby arugula in the salad. Or simply serve the
salad on some greens and enjoy.

KALE AND FALAFEL SALAD WITH TAHINI DRESSING

SERVES 4 · · (30)

A combination of falafel and kale comes together with the creamy tahini dressing. This restaurant favorite is easy to make at home and can make any weeknight a fun night in.

TAHINI DRESSING

1/4 cup (60 mL) tahini

3 tbsp (45 mL) water

2 tbsp (30 mL) lemon juice

1 tbsp (15 mL) maple syrup

1 tbsp (15 mL) chopped fresh parsley

1 tsp (5 mL) sesame oil

1/4 tsp (1 mL) each salt and black pepper

KALE SALAD

12 falafels (store-bought or homemade)

6 cups (1.5 L) chopped kale leaves

1 tbsp (15 mL) lemon juice

1/2 tsp (2 mL) salt

1 cup (250 mL) grape tomatoes, halved

1 cup (250 mL) thinly sliced cucumber

1/2 cup (125 mL) sliced almonds, toasted

1 TAHINI DRESSING: In a small bowl, whisk together tahini, water, lemon juice, maple syrup, parsley, sesame oil, salt and pepper until smooth; set aside.

2 Preheat oven to 350°F (180°C).

3 KALE SALAD: Place falafels on baking sheet and warm through for about 5 minutes or according to package directions.

4 Meanwhile, in a large bowl, rub kale with lemon juice and salt until slightly wilted. Toss with half of the Tahini Dressing. Add tomatoes, cucumbers and almonds.

5 Divide among plates and top with falafels. Drizzle salads with remaining Tahini Dressing to serve.

TIP

You can make falafels from a mix that comes in boxes or look for them premade in refrigerated and freezer sections of larger grocery stores.

POACHED EGG AND GREENS WINTER SALAD

SERVES 2 · (30) · 🌿

Eggs are easy and make a wonderful dinner salad,
especially with a friend.

1/4 cup (60 mL) canola oil, divided

2 slices sourdough bread, cubed

3/4 tsp (3 mL) salt, divided

1/4 tsp (1 mL) dried Italian seasoning

1 package (10 oz/300 g) baby kale

1 red bell pepper, thinly sliced

1/2 tsp (2 mL) black pepper

2 large eggs

Hot pepper sauce or Sriracha for drizzling

1 In a large skillet, heat 2 tbsp (30 mL) of the oil over medium heat. Add bread, 1/4 tsp (1 mL) of the salt and Italian seasoning; sauté for about 8 minutes or until golden. Scrape into a bowl.

2 Return skillet to medium-high heat and add remaining oil. Sauté kale, red pepper and remaining salt and pepper for about 5 minutes or until wilted. Divide among two dinner plates and sprinkle each with croutons.

3 Meanwhile, bring a pot of water to simmer. Gently crack 1 egg into a small bowl and lower into water. Repeat with remaining egg. Cook eggs for about 3 minutes or until desired doneness. Remove poached eggs with slotted spoon and place 1 on top of each salad plate. Drizzle with sauce to serve.

TIP

For a heartier salad, double up the eggs for each serving.

ASIAN COLESLAW WITH CHICKEN

MAKES 6 TO 8 SERVINGS · · ·

A refreshing crunchy cabbage salad inspired by Vietnamese and Thai flavors. Toasting the almonds and coconut adds a delicious nutty flavor and texture. The dressing and salad can be made a few hours ahead and stored in the refrigerator. Almonds, coconut, cilantro and green onion are added just before serving to maintain their texture and fresh flavor.

DRESSING

3 tbsp (45 mL) lime juice

2 garlic cloves, minced

1 tbsp (15 mL) canola oil

1 tbsp (15 mL) fish sauce

1 tbsp (15 mL) packed light brown sugar

1 tsp (5 mL) chili garlic sauce

SALAD

¼ cup (60 mL) unsweetened shredded coconut

¼ cup (60 mL) slivered almonds

5 cups (1.25 L) coleslaw mix

2 cups (500 mL) shredded cooked chicken

1 red bell pepper, cut into thin strips

½ English cucumber, sliced

1 cup (250 mL) chopped fresh cilantro

1 green onion, finely sliced

1 DRESSING: In a small jar, combine lime juice, garlic, oil, fish sauce, sugar and chili garlic sauce. Cover and refrigerate until ready to use.

2 SALAD: In small skillet, over medium-low heat, add coconut. Stir frequently until coconut is golden brown. Transfer to plate to cool. Repeat with almonds in the same skillet. Transfer to plate to cool.

3 Meanwhile, in a large bowl, combine coleslaw mix, chicken, red pepper and cucumber. Drizzle with half of the dressing, tossing to coat.

4 Just before serving, add cilantro, almonds, coconut and green onion, adding more dressing to taste. Serve immediately.

TIPS

Toast the almonds and coconut up to 3 days ahead.

Substitute half of the cilantro with chopped mint.

MEXICAN STREET CORN AND TURKEY SALAD

SERVES 4 ·

Grilled corn and turkey come together for a new spin on a summer favorite. Enjoy this salad warm or cold. For some fun, add a sprinkle of crushed tortilla chips on top!

CILANTRO DRESSING

1/4 cup (60 mL) light mayonnaise

2 tbsp (30 mL) cider vinegar

1/2 tsp (2 mL) chili powder

Pinch salt

2 tbsp (30 mL) chopped fresh cilantro

CORN AND TURKEY SALAD

1 boneless skinless turkey breast (about 1 lb/500 g)

2 tbsp (30 mL) canola oil

1/2 tsp (2 mL) grated lime zest

2 tbsp (30 mL) lime juice

1 tsp (5 mL) ground cumin

1/2 tsp (2 mL) each salt and pepper

4 cobs of corn, shucked

1 cup (250 mL) crumbled feta cheese

1/2 cup (125 mL) diced red onion

2 tbsp (30 mL) chopped fresh cilantro

1 CILANTRO DRESSING: In a small bowl, whisk together mayonnaise, vinegar, chili powder and salt until smooth. Stir in cilantro; cover and refrigerate until ready to use.

2 CORN AND TURKEY SALAD: Using a chef's knife, remove tenderloin from turkey breast. Hold knife horizontally in center of turkey breast and cut in half; you should have 2 equal-size pieces. Place all 3 of the turkey pieces into a large shallow dish or resealable plastic bag.

3 In a small bowl, whisk together oil, lime zest and lime juice, cumin, salt and pepper. Pour over turkey and turn to coat well. Let stand for at least 10 minutes or cover and refrigerate for up to 12 hours.

4 Preheat grill to medium-high heat.

5 Spray corn cobs lightly with cooking spray and place on grill. Close lid and grill, turning occasionally, for about 10 minutes or until golden. Remove to cutting board to cool slightly.

6 Meanwhile, place turkey breasts on grill. Close lid and grill for about 5 minutes or until edges are golden. Turn over and grill for about 5 minutes or until turkey is no longer pink inside and juices run clear. Remove from grill.

7 Cut off kernels from corn and place in a large bowl. Chop turkey into bite-size pieces and add to corn. Add feta, onion and cilantro. Pour over Cilantro Dressing and stir gently to coat.

TIP
Cover and refrigerate for up to 2 days.

Vegetable puns make me feel good from my head to-ma-toes.

AVOCADO SHRIMP SALAD

SERVES 6 ·

A creamy yogurt dressing adds zing to the combination of smoky shrimp and crunchy greens. Celebrate a job well done with this beautiful salad.

HERB YOGURT DRESSING

1/3 cup (75 mL) Balkan-style plain yogurt

2 tbsp (30 mL) canola oil

1 tbsp (15 mL) lemon juice

1/2 tsp (2 mL) salt

1/4 tsp (1 mL) dry mustard

3 tbsp (45 mL) finely chopped fresh basil

1 tbsp (15 mL) chopped fresh parsley

AVOCADO SHRIMP SALAD

2 tbsp (30 mL) canola oil

1 package (16 oz/454 g) jumbo raw black tiger shrimp, peeled and deveined

1 tsp (5 mL) smoked paprika

1 garlic clove, minced

1/2 tsp (2 mL) grated lime zest

4 cups (1 L) chopped romaine

2 cups (500 mL) grape tomatoes

1 large avocado, thinly sliced

1/4 cup (60 mL) coarsely chopped red onion (optional)

1 HERB YOGURT DRESSING: In a bowl, whisk together yogurt, oil, lemon juice, salt, mustard, basil and parsley; set aside.

2 AVOCADO SHRIMP SALAD: Heat oil in a large skillet over medium-high heat. Add shrimp, paprika, garlic and lime zest; cook, stirring for about 5 minutes or until shrimp are cooked through. Remove from heat.

3 Spread lettuce onto a platter and top with tomatoes, avocado and red onion, if using. Top with shrimp and serve Herb Yogurt Dressing alongside.

TIP

Use a ripe but firm avocado for best flavor and color. Choose firm avocados a few days ahead of using them, so they ripen perfectly for you at home.

BEEF AND VEAL

❦

BEEF AND CABBAGE SKILLET NOODLES

SERVES 4 TO 6 · ·

One-skillet meals are always a great way to celebrate a great day in school or at the office. This version comes together easily and the kids will be happy to get cooking so they can add those crunchy noodles at the end!

1 tbsp (15 mL) canola oil

1 lb (500 g) ground beef or veal

1 shallot, finely chopped

1 large garlic clove, minced

1 tbsp (15 mL) minced fresh ginger

1/4 cup (60 mL) soy sauce

3 tbsp (45 mL) light brown sugar

1 tbsp (15 mL) sesame oil

1 bag (14 oz/397 g) coleslaw mix

1/2 tsp (2 mL) Sriracha

3 cups (750 mL) crispy (fried) chow mein noodles

1 In a large nonstick skillet, heat oil over medium-high heat. Add beef, shallot, garlic and ginger and cook, breaking up beef, for about 5 minutes or until browned.

2 Stir in soy sauce, brown sugar and sesame oil. Add coleslaw and Sriracha and cook, stirring about 4 minutes or until coleslaw wilts. Add chow mein noodles and stir until well coated.

TIP

Emily's friend Rani served her leftovers of this noodle dish in lettuce wraps as a fun appetizer idea. With a drizzle of Sriracha over top, guests wanted more! We always love a recipe that plays double duty.

JALAPEÑO CHEESE BURGERS

SERVES 6 ·

Here's a burger recipe you'll want on repeat!
You're in the driver's seat in controlling how much heat goes
into this burger. For less jalapeño heat, reduce or discard
the seeds and interior pepper "ribs." It's also a good idea to
wear gloves when handling fresh jalapeño. Serve with a
side of salad and French fries or potato chips.

SPICY MAYONNAISE

1/4 cup (60 mL) mayonnaise

2 tbsp (30 mL) finely chopped pickled jalapeños, drained

2 tbsp (30 mL) ketchup

1 tsp (5 mL) granulated sugar

BURGERS

1/4 cup (60 mL) dry bread crumbs

1/2 small onion, grated

1 jalapeño, finely chopped

1 garlic clove, minced

1 tbsp (15 mL) Worcestershire sauce

2 tsp (10 mL) Montreal-style steak spice

1 1/2 lbs (750 g) lean ground beef or veal

6 slices extra-sharp (extra-old) Cheddar cheese

6 slices cooked bacon

6 hamburger buns

Lettuce leaves

Tomato slices

1 SPICY MAYONNAISE: In a small bowl, combine spicy mayonnaise ingredients. Cover and store in refrigerator until ready to use.

2 BURGERS: In a large bowl, add bread crumbs, onion, jalapeño, garlic, Worcestershire and steak spice; stir to combine. Add beef and mix gently until well combined. Gently shape mixture into six 4-inch (10 cm) patties, about 3/4-inch (2 cm) thick. Place on a baking tray and make an indentation in the center of each patty for even cooking; refrigerate 10 minutes.

3 Meanwhile, preheat barbecue grill to medium-high. Place patties on greased grill and grill for 4 to 5 minutes per side or until no longer pink inside and a meat thermometer inserted horizontally in the center of the patty registers 160°F (71°C).

4 Turn grill off and lay a slice of cheese and bacon on top of each patty; close lid. Remove patties when cheese is just beginning to melt, after about 30 seconds. Serve with spicy mayonnaise, buns, lettuce and tomato slices.

TIP
Jalapeño Jack cheese can be substituted for the Cheddar cheese.

HEART-SHAPE MINI MEATLOAVES

SERVES 4 TO 6 ·

Emily has been making these meatloaves since her kids were little. The kids would recognize Valentine's Day as Love Day, and this was the perfect way to shape one of their favorite dishes into hearts. If you have a heart-shaped cookie cutter, be sure to cut out hearts from potatoes and roast them to serve alongside.

1/3 cup (75 mL) dry seasoned bread crumbs

3 tbsp (45 mL) grated Parmesan cheese

1 large egg, lightly beaten

1/2 cup (125 mL) pasta or pizza sauce, divided

1/2 tsp (2 mL) salt

1/4 tsp (1 mL) black pepper

1 small onion, grated or finely diced

1/3 cup (75 mL) finely diced red or green bell pepper (optional)

2 garlic cloves, minced

1 tsp (5 mL) dried oregano

1 lb (500 g) extra lean ground beef or veal

1/3 cup (75 mL) shredded mozzarella cheese (optional)

1 Preheat oven to 400°F (200°C). Line a baking sheet with parchment paper; set aside.

2 In a large bowl, combine bread crumbs, cheese, egg, 1/4 cup (60 mL) of the pasta sauce, salt and pepper. Stir in onion, red pepper, if using, garlic and oregano. Add beef and stir to combine well.

3 Divide mixture evenly into 6 balls and shape into hearts about 1-inch (2.5 cm) thick. Place on prepared baking sheet. Top each with remaining sauce and cheese, if using. Bake for about 20 minutes or until an inserted thermometer reaches 160°F (71°C). Let stand 2 minutes before serving.

MAKE AHEAD

Shape the meatloaves and cover baking sheet and refrigerate for up to 8 hours before baking.

ONE-POT BEEFY TOMATO MACARONI DINNER

SERVES 5 ·

This favorite comfort meal is a big hit with Sylvia's family. With ground beef and mushrooms in a creamy sauce, this tasty dish is bound to become one of your family favorites, too.

2 tsp (10 mL) canola oil

1 lb (500 g) lean ground beef or veal

1 onion, finely chopped

1½ cups (375 mL) sliced mushrooms

1 carrot, finely chopped

1 garlic clove, minced

2 tsp (10 mL) mustard

1 tsp (5 mL) hot sauce

½ tsp (2 mL) each salt and black pepper

1½ cups (375 mL) ready-to-use beef broth

1 can (28 oz/796 mL) diced tomatoes

1½ cups (375 mL) dried elbow macaroni pasta

1½ cups (375 mL) shredded Cheddar cheese

½ cup (125 mL) sour cream

1 In a large pot, heat oil over medium-high heat; add beef and onion. Cook, breaking meat into small pieces, about 5 minutes. Add mushrooms, carrot, garlic, mustard, hot sauce, salt and pepper and cook another 5 minutes, stirring frequently.

2 Add broth and tomatoes, cover and bring to boil. Stir in macaroni, then reduce heat to medium and cover. Stir occasionally. Cook about 20 minutes or until macaroni is al dente. Remove from heat and stir in cheese.

3 Top each serving with a dollop of sour cream and serve with extra hot sauce on the side.

TIP
Chop and the vegetables and grate the cheese the night before to get a head start on the meal preparation.

INSTANT POT PAPRIKA BEEF STEW

SERVES 6 ·

This rich flavorful beef stew is seasoned with two kinds of paprika and a bit of caraway seed. Serve over rice, mashed potatoes, hot cooked egg noodles or crusty rolls. The stew is a perfect make-ahead meal as it reheats well.

2 tbsp (30 mL) canola oil

1 onion, chopped

2 lbs (1 kg) boneless beef chuck roast or veal, cut into 1-inch (2.5 cm) cubes

1 tsp (5 mL) each salt and black pepper

3 large carrots, chopped

2 tbsp (30 mL) sweet paprika

2 tsp (10 mL) smoked paprika

¼ cup (60 mL) tomato paste

2 garlic cloves, minced

1 tsp (5 mL) dried thyme

2 tsp (10 mL) caraway seeds

1 bay leaf

1½ cups (375 mL) ready-to-use beef broth

2 tbsp (30 mL) water

2 tbsp (30 mL) cornstarch

Sour cream

1 In a 6-quart Instant Pot, select Sauté. Add oil and onion; cook 5 minutes, stirring occasionally. Add beef; sprinkle with salt and pepper and sauté 5 minutes, stirring occasionally. Add carrots, sweet paprika, smoked paprika, tomato paste, garlic, thyme, caraway seeds and bay leaf; stir to combine. Stir in beef broth.

2 Press Cancel and lock lid; set pressure release valve to Sealing. Press Manual Pressure Cook; set to High for 25 minutes. (It takes about 10 minutes to come to pressure.) When cooking finishes; let the pressure release naturally for 20 minutes, then release any remaining steam by moving the pressure release valve to Venting. Press Cancel; open lid, select Sauté.

3 In a small bowl, combine water and cornstarch; stir into stew. Bring to a simmer, cooking until stew thickens slightly, about 5 minutes. Press Cancel. Top each serving with a dollop of sour cream.

TIP
Freeze unused tomato paste in 1 tbsp (15 mL) portions on a parchment paper lined pan. Freeze until solid, then transfer to a freezer-safe container. Freeze until ready to use.

TERIYAKI FAUX RIBS AND KIMCHI RICE

SERVES 2

Create boneless beef ribs from steak easily
by slicing it up and making this fun meal for two.

2 cups (500 mL) ready-
to-use beef or vegetable
broth

1 cup (250 mL) sushi
(Calrose) rice

2 tbsp (30 mL) rice vinegar

1 striploin steak (about
8 oz/250 g)

1/2 cup (125 mL) teriyaki
or kalbi sauce, divided

2 tbsp (30 mL) canola oil

3/4 cup (175 mL) kimchi,
chopped

2 green onions, chopped

1/2 cup (125 mL) shredded
carrot

1/4 cup (60 mL) diced
cucumber (optional)

1 In a saucepan, stir together broth and rice. Bring to a simmer over medium-high heat. Reduce heat to low; cover and cook for about 15 minutes or until broth is absorbed and rice is tender. Stir in rice vinegar; set aside.

2 Trim any excess fat from steak and cut crosswise into 1/2-inch (1 cm) strips; place in a bowl. Add half of the teriyaki sauce and stir to coat well; let stand for 10 minutes.

3 In a skillet over medium-high heat, cook steak strips, turning occasionally, for about 5 minutes or until hint of pink remains.

4 Meanwhile, heat oil in a large nonstick skillet over medium-high heat. Sauté rice, kimchi and green onions, stirring often, for 6 minutes or until heated through.

5 Divide rice on plates and top with ribs. Drizzle with remaining teriyaki sauce and top with carrot and cucumber if using.

TIP

Be sure to serve more of the kimchi for those who want an added kick of crunch and heat.

GRILLED PARTY STEAK WITH TOMATILLO AVOCADO SALSA

SERVES 6 TO 8 · ·

Why grill many steaks when one steak will feed the gang?
This party-size steak is perfect sliced up for sharing with
family and friends. Adding flavor and texture with
the salsa makes it irresistible.

SALSA

4 tomatillos, husked and quartered

2 small garlic cloves

2 jalapeño peppers, seeded and halved

1 avocado, chopped

1/3 cup (75 mL) ready-to-use vegetable broth or water

2 tbsp (30 mL) lime juice

1/3 cup (75 mL) chopped fresh cilantro

Salt

PARTY STEAK

2 tbsp (30 mL) extra virgin olive oil

2 tbsp (30 mL) each chopped fresh parsley, chives and mint

2 tsp (10 mL) chopped fresh thyme

1/2 tsp (2 mL) each salt and black pepper

Pinch hot pepper flakes

1 top beef sirloin grilling steak, about 1-inch (2.5 cm) thick (about 2 lb/1 kg), trimmed

1 TOMATILLO AVOCADO SALSA: Place tomatillos, garlic and jalapeño peppers in a food processor and pulse until coarsely chopped. Add avocado, broth and lime juice and purée until almost smooth. Stir in cilantro and salt to taste. Refrigerate until ready to serve.

2 PARTY STEAK: In a bowl, combine oil, parsley, chives, mint, thyme, salt, pepper and hot pepper flakes. Spread herb mixture all over steak.

3 Preheat grill to medium-high heat. Grill steak, turning occasionally for about 10 minutes or until thermometer reaches 135°F (57°C) or until desired doneness. Remove to a cutting board and cover with foil. Let rest for 10 minutes. Slice thinly across the grain and serve with tomatillo avocado salsa.

CAST-IRON SKILLET/OVEN VARIATION

Heat cast-iron skillet over medium-high heat. Brown steak on both sides and place steak and pan in 400°F (200°C) oven for about 10 minutes or until it reaches desired doneness. Cover with aluminum foil and let rest for 10 minutes.

CRANBERRY THYME OVEN BRISKET

SERVES 10 TO 12 · ·

Our close friend and fellow cookbook author Daphna Rabinovitch shared her make-ahead cranberry-infused brisket recipe. It is perfect to serve with a big pile of mashed potatoes! This recipe absorbs all the flavor of the sauce because it chills overnight and is reheated in the sauce the next day.

2 tbsp (30 mL) canola oil

6 garlic cloves, chopped

2 onions, coarsely chopped

2 leeks, white part only, coarsely chopped

2 carrots, coarsely chopped

1 cup (250 mL) cranberry cocktail

1 can (12.25 oz/348 mL) cranberry sauce

1 cup (250 mL) ready-to-use beef or chicken broth

2 bay leaves

2 tsp (10 mL) dried thyme

1 tsp (5 mL) dried rosemary, crushed

3/4 tsp (3 mL) salt

1/4 tsp (1 mL) cayenne pepper

1/2 tsp (2 mL) black pepper

1 beef brisket, trimmed of excess fat (about 4 lb/2 kg)

1. In a large skillet, heat oil over medium heat. Sauté garlic, onions, leeks and carrots for about 10 minutes or until softened. Add cranberry cocktail, scraping up any browned bits from the bottom of the pot, and bring to a boil. Boil for about 5 minutes or until most of the juice has been absorbed. Stir in cranberry sauce and broth; bring to a boil. Add bay leaves and remove from heat.

2. Preheat oven to 325°F (160°C). In a small bowl, combine thyme, rosemary, salt, cayenne and pepper; rub over both sides of brisket. Place brisket, fat side up, in a large roasting pan. Pour vegetable mixture over brisket, lifting meat to ensure the sauce goes underneath as well. Cover pan tightly with foil. Roast for 3 to 3 1/2 hours or until beef is very tender. Uncover to let cool to room temperature. Cover and refrigerate overnight.

3. Preheat oven to 325°F (160°C). Gently remove any congealed fat from the pan and discard bay leaves. Transfer meat to a cutting board. Pour vegetables and pan juices into a food processor and purée until smooth. Pour back into the pan. Slice meat across the grain, then nestle slices into the sauce. Cover pan with foil and roast for at least 1 hour or until heated through.

BEEF WELLINGTON PACKAGES FOR EVERYONE

SERVES 8

Emily's good friend Amy developed this recipe years ago and it has been a favorite for Emily's son Matthew to make every holiday season since! Everyone is happy when they get to cut into their own little dinner package.

2 tbsp (30 mL) canola oil, divided

2 tbsp (30 mL) butter

2 shallots, chopped

12 oz (375 g) cremini or white mushrooms, chopped

1 tsp (5 mL) dried thyme

1 tsp (5 mL) each salt and black pepper, divided

1/3 cup (75 mL) dry white wine

8 beef tenderloin medallions (about 4 oz/125 g each)

1 tbsp (15 mL) Dijon mustard

8 slices prosciutto

1 package (1 lb/450 g) puff pastry sheets

1 large egg, beaten

Horseradish (optional)

1 In a large skillet, heat 1 tbsp (15 mL) of the oil with the butter over medium heat. Add shallots, mushrooms, thyme and half each of the salt and pepper. Sauté for about 8 minutes or until mushrooms are browned. Add wine and simmer for 5 minutes or until all the liquid is absorbed. Spread out on a plate to cool.

2 Wipe out the pan; add the remaining oil. Return to medium-high heat. Season the beef medallions with remaining salt and pepper. Add beef to the hot skillet, in batches if necessary, and brown well on both sides. Transfer to a rack to cool.

3 Preheat oven to 400°F (200°C). Line a baking sheet with parchment paper; set aside.

4 Lay the slices of prosciutto out on a work surface. Spread Dijon evenly over one side of each slice of prosciutto. Place an equal portion of the mushroom mixture in the center of each piece of prosciutto. Top each with a cooled beef medallion and bring the sides of the prosciutto up over the steak to enclose.

5 Unroll each sheet of puff pastry onto a lightly floured surface. Roll out gently to make two 14-inch (35 cm) squares. Cut each square into four 7-inch (18 cm) squares. Place a beef medallion, mushroom-side-down, in the center of each square. Brush the edges with egg. Bring opposing corners of the pastry up to overlap, pinching the seams to seal. Place seam-side-down on prepared pan. Brush with additional egg wash.

6 Roast for 20 to 25 minutes or until an instant-read thermometer inserted into the meat registers 140°F (60°C). Let rest for 10 minutes before serving.

MAKE AHEAD

Mushroom mixture can be made ahead and held in the refrigerator for up to 1 day.

After the pastry squares are filled and prepared, you can cover with plastic wrap and refrigerate for up to 6 hours. Let stand at room temperature for 30 minutes before roasting.

TIP

If you prefer, you can substitute 4 striploin or ribeye steaks, cut in half crosswise, as they are a similar size to 1-inch (2.5 cm) thick medallions. Be sure to trim any excess fat before searing them.

Why do hamburgers go to the gym?
To get better buns!

HEARTY RAGU PAPPARDELLE

SERVES 6 TO 8

Some winter afternoons you want a hearty meat sauce simmering away to fill your home with an amazing aroma to celebrate that snow-plowed driveway. This will fill your belly and more.

3 tbsp (45 mL) canola oil

2½ lbs (1.25 kg) stewing veal or beef

¼ tsp (1 mL) each salt and black pepper

2 celery stalks, diced

1 large carrot, diced

1 large onion, diced

2 cups (500 mL) red wine

4 cups (1 L) ready-to-use beef broth

2½ cups (625 mL) passata (strained tomatoes)

4 garlic cloves, minced

1 tbsp (15 mL) finely chopped fresh rosemary or 1 tsp (5 mL) dried

1 tbsp (15 mL) finely chopped fresh thyme or 1 tsp (5 mL) dried

Salt and black pepper

1 lb (500 g) dried pappardelle pasta

Parmesan shavings

1 In a large Dutch oven, heat oil over medium-high heat. Sprinkle veal with salt and pepper and brown veal cubes, in batches; remove to a bowl. Reduce heat to medium; add celery, carrot and onion. Cook, stirring, for about 5 minutes or until lightly browned. Increase heat to high. Add wine; cook, scraping up brown bits from bottom of pan, for about 5 minutes or until reduced by about half. Add broth and passata.

2 Return browned veal and accumulated juices to pan and return to a simmer. Reduce heat; cover and simmer for about 2 hours or until veal is very tender. Uncover and add garlic, rosemary and thyme. Cook on medium-high for about 30 minutes, stirring often, or until thickened. Season with additional salt and pepper to taste if needed.

3 In a large pot of boiling salted water, cook pasta for about 8 minutes or until al dente. Drain well. Toss with ragu. Sprinkle with cheese to serve.

TIPS

You can make the ragu up to 3 days ahead. Warm through over low heat before tossing with the pappardelle.

Have a smaller household? No problem; divide the portions and freeze them for up to 1 month to enjoy later.

OVEN VARIATION

If you want to cook the ragu in the oven, once everything is back in the pot, cover and cook in a 350°F (180°C) oven for about 2½ hours. Stir in garlic, rosemary and thyme and simmer uncovered on the stovetop to thicken slightly.

JILLIAN'S FAVORITE AUSSIE BEEF MEAT PIES

SERVES 8 ·

Meat pies are a big hit with Sylvia's family, especially for her daughter. This iconic Australian meat pie is traditionally served with ketchup and uses two types of pastry. The meat filling is surrounded by tender pastry and topped with a puff pastry lid. You can use store-bought pie pastry and puff pastry or go the homemade route.

1 tbsp (15 mL) canola oil

1 onion, diced

2 carrots, diced

2 cups (500 mL) mushrooms, quartered

2 garlic cloves, minced

2 tbsp (30 mL) Worcestershire sauce

1 tbsp (15 mL) tomato paste

1 tsp (5 mL) each salt and black pepper

$\frac{1}{4}$ tsp (1 mL) grated nutmeg

$1\frac{1}{2}$ lbs (750 g) stewing beef or veal, cut into $\frac{1}{2}$-inch (1 cm) cubes

$\frac{1}{2}$ cup (125 mL) ready-to-use beef broth

$\frac{1}{2}$ cup (125 mL) red wine

2 tbsp (30 mL) cornstarch

2 tbsp (30 mL) water

1 In a large heavy pot, heat oil over medium-high heat; sauté onion until soft, about 5 minutes, stirring occasionally. Add carrot, mushrooms, garlic, Worcestershire, tomato paste, salt, pepper, nutmeg and beef; cook, stirring, for 5 minutes.

2 Add beef stock and wine, bring to a boil, then reduce heat to low. Cover, and cook for $1\frac{1}{4}$ hours or until beef is tender.

3 In a small bowl, combine cornstarch and water and stir into beef mixture; cook for 5 minutes to thicken the sauce. Remove pot from stove and set aside; cool to room temperature.

4 When ready to bake, preheat oven to 425°F (220°C). Move oven rack to the lowest position. Lightly grease eight 5-inch (12.5 cm) pie tins. On a lightly floured surface, roll out pie pastry and cut eight 6-inch (15 cm) circles.

5 Line the inside of each pie tin with pie pastry. In a small bowl, whisk together egg and water, then lightly brush the top edge of pastry with egg wash. Spoon the cooled meat filling into the pie shells.

Pastry for a double-crust
 pie

1 recipe for Easy Puff
 Pastry (see page 54)

1 large egg, lightly beaten

1 tbsp (15 mL) water

6 On a lightly floured surface, roll out puff pastry into two 10-inch (25 cm) squares. From each piece of pastry, cut out four 5-inch (12.5 cm) rounds. Top each pie with a round of puff pastry. Press and crimp the edges to seal. Brush the top of each pie with egg wash, then make a small slit into the top of each for a steam vent.

7 Place pies on a rimmed baking sheet and bake on bottom rack for 20 minutes. Reduce the oven temperature to 375°F (190°C) and bake an additional 20 minutes, or until the pastry is golden brown. Transfer pies to a rack to cool slightly before serving.

MAKE AHEAD

The beef filling can be made 2 days in advance. Store in an airtight container in the refrigerator.

The baked pies freeze well for up to 2 months.

TIP

If you want the convenience of store-bought puff pastry, use a 1-lb (450 g) package.

How do you make a gold pie?
You put 14 carrots in it.

VEAL TACOS WITH SUN-DRIED TOMATO TOMATILLO SAUCE

SERVES 4

This twist on a family favorite is delicious with or without tortillas!

SUN-DRIED TOMATO TOMATILLO SAUCE

1 tbsp (15 mL) canola oil

1/2 cup (125 mL) diced red onion

1 large garlic clove, minced

2 tomatillos, husked and diced

3 tbsp (45 mL) lime juice

1/2 tsp (2 mL) hot pepper sauce

1/4 tsp (1 mL) salt

1/4 cup (60 mL) sour cream

2 tbsp (30 mL) finely chopped sun-dried tomatoes, drained

VEAL TACOS

3/4 cup (175 mL) seasoned bread crumbs

2 tbsp (30 mL) chopped fresh parsley

1/2 tsp (2 mL) each garlic powder and onion powder

1/4 tsp (1 mL) black pepper

1 large egg

12 oz (375 g) veal or beef cutlets or scaloppine

3 tbsp (45 mL) canola oil

6 small flour or corn tortillas, warmed

1 SUN-DRIED TOMATO TOMATILLO SAUCE: In a skillet, heat oil over medium heat. Cook onion and garlic for 2 minutes or until softened. Add tomatillos and cook, stirring for 3 minutes or until softened. Remove from heat and stir in lime juice, hot pepper sauce and salt. Stir in sour cream and tomatoes; cover and refrigerate.

2 VEAL TACOS: In a shallow bowl, combine bread crumbs, parsley, garlic powder, onion powder and pepper. Whisk egg in another bowl. Coat cutlets in egg and let excess drip off. Coat both sides evenly with bread-crumb mixture and place on parchment paper lined baking sheet.

3 In a large nonstick skillet, heat oil over medium-high heat and cook cutlets for about 3 minutes per side or until golden brown and hint of pink remains inside. Cut into strips.

4 Place strips into warmed tortillas and top with Sun-Dried Tomato Tomatillo Sauce to serve.

TIP

If using canned tomatillos, be sure to freeze any unused tomatillos so you can make the sauce again for an addition to any of your taco nights.

CHICKEN AND TURKEY

~

THAI CHICKEN STIR-FRY

SERVES 2 · 🕐 30

This is our quick and easy-to-prepare version of a popular Thai take-out meal. If Thai basil is not available, use sweet basil as a substitute. The sweet basil will not have that special aniseed flavor, but will still taste satisfying and delicious. Serve with hot cooked rice or noodles.

SAUCE

1/4 cup (60 mL) water

1 tbsp (15 mL) oyster sauce

1 tbsp (15 mL) fish sauce

1 tsp (5 mL) granulated sugar

1 tsp (5 mL) chili garlic sauce

1 tsp (5 mL) cornstarch

1/2 tsp (2 mL) soy sauce

CHICKEN STIR-FRY

2 tbsp (30 mL) canola oil

1/2 small onion, cut into thin slices

1/2 lb (250 g) chicken thighs, cut into 1/4-inch (0.5 cm) strips

2 garlic cloves, minced

1 red bell pepper, cut into thin strips

1 cup (250 mL) snap peas

1 green onion, sliced

1/3 cup (75 mL) lightly packed Thai basil leaves

1 SAUCE: In a small bowl, combine sauce ingredients; set aside.

2 CHICKEN STIR-FRY: In a large skillet, heat oil over medium-high heat; add onion and cook 2 minutes, stirring occasionally. Stir in chicken and garlic and cook 1 minute. Add red pepper, peas, green onion and sauce mixture; cook 3 to 4 minutes, stirring occasionally, until chicken is cooked through and vegetables are tender crisp.

3 Remove from heat and stir in basil. Serve over rice or noodles.

TIP

To get a head start on cooking, prepare the sauce the night before, cover and refrigerate. You can also chop the onion, chicken, bell pepper and green onions; cover and refrigerate.

MANGO CHIPOTLE CHICKEN SKEWERS

SERVES 6 · ·  ·

The subtle fruity flavor of this barbecue sauce makes a tasty change from classic barbecue sauce and adds a sweet, smoky, tangy touch of the tropics to these grilled chicken skewers. Serve with a side of coleslaw and buns.

MANGO CHIPOTLE BARBECUE SAUCE

1 mango, peeled, pitted and chopped

3/4 cup (175 mL) ketchup

3 tbsp (45 mL) packed brown sugar

1/3 cup (75 mL) balsamic vinegar

3 garlic cloves, minced

1 chipotle pepper in adobo sauce

1 lime, juiced

1 tbsp (15 mL) canola oil

1 tsp (5 mL) salt

CHICKEN

1 1/2 lbs (750 g) boneless, skinless chicken breasts, cut into 1-inch (2.5 cm) cubes

1 red onion, cut into 1-inch (2.5 cm) squares

Lime wedges

Chopped fresh cilantro (optional)

1 MANGO CHIPOTLE BARBECUE SAUCE: In a blender, combine mango, ketchup, brown sugar, vinegar, garlic, chipotle pepper, lime juice, oil and salt; purée until smooth. Transfer to a saucepan over medium heat. Cook 5 minutes until it begins to thicken; partially cover with a lid if it starts to splatter.

2 Cool to room temperature. (You can refrigerate sauce in an airtight container for up to 1 week.) Makes about 2 cups (500 mL).

3 CHICKEN: In a bowl, place chicken, onions and 1/2 cup (125 mL) of the barbecue sauce; stir to fully coat. Cover and refrigerate for up to 1 hour.

4 Meanwhile, preheat barbecue grill to medium-high. Thread the chicken and onions onto skewers, discarding marinade in bowl. Place skewers on a greased grill. Grill, turning occasionally for about 10 to 12 minutes or until chicken is cooked through.

5 Serve with lime wedges, a sprinkle of cilantro, if using, and extra barbecue sauce on the side.

TIP

Chipotle peppers in adobo sauce are canned, smoked and dried jalapeño peppers.

TIPS

If using bamboo skewers, soak in water for at least 30 minutes before using.

Use extra barbecue sauce for brushing onto other grilled or roasted meats, burgers or meatloaf. It's also a tasty dip for meatballs and chicken wings. Store in the refrigerator for up to 1 week, or freeze for up to 2 months.

You can substitute $1\frac{1}{2}$ cups (375 mL) frozen chopped mango for the fresh mango. Thaw before proceeding with recipe.

Why did it take the chicken so long to cross the road? There was no eggs-press lane!

HUMMUS SOUVLAKI CHICKEN BURGERS

SERVES 4 ·

Switch up your chicken souvlaki from skewers to burgers! With this fresh tasting hummus sauce, it will taste like summer on your plate.

ROASTED PEPPER FETA HUMMUS SAUCE

1/2 cup (125 mL) hummus

1/2 cup (125 mL) roasted red pepper

1/4 cup (60 mL) crumbled feta cheese

2 tbsp (30 mL) chopped fresh parsley

SOUVLAKI BURGERS

2 boneless skinless chicken breasts

3 tbsp (45 mL) canola oil

2 garlic cloves, minced

1/2 tsp (2 mL) grated lemon zest

2 tbsp (30 mL) lemon juice

1 tsp (5 mL) dried oregano

1/4 tsp (1 mL) each salt and black pepper

4 burger buns

1 cup (250 mL) torn romaine lettuce

Sliced cucumbers

1 ROASTED PEPPER FETA HUMMUS SAUCE: In a small food processor, combine hummus and roasted red peppers; purée until smooth. Stir in feta and parsley; set aside or cover and refrigerate until ready to use.

2 SOUVLAKI BURGERS: Slice chicken breasts in half horizontally to get 4 equal pieces of chicken. In a shallow dish, whisk together oil, garlic, lemon zest, lemon juice, oregano, salt and pepper. Add chicken and turn to coat well. Let stand for 15 minutes or cover and refrigerate for up to 4 hours.

3 Preheat grill to medium heat. Place chicken on greased grill, turning occasionally, for about 10 minutes or until no longer pink inside and thermometer registers 165°F (74°C).

4 Spread some of the Roasted Pepper Feta Hummus sauce on the bottom buns and top with lettuce, then grilled chicken. Spread with more sauce and top with cucumbers. Add top bun and serve.

VARIATION

Substitute 1 tub (8 oz/227 g) roasted red pepper hummus for the hummus and roasted red pepper for a quick shortcut.

BONELESS CHICKEN CACCIATORE

SERVES 6 ·

Chicken Cacciatore, or "hunter's chicken," offers up the chunky pieces of vegetables and chicken that are favorites for adults and kids alike. Enjoy with rice, pasta or on its own.

2 lbs (1 kg) boneless skinless chicken thighs

¼ tsp (1 mL) each salt and black pepper

2 tbsp (30 mL) extra virgin olive oil, divided

1 onion, chopped

4 garlic cloves, minced

1 lb (500 g) mushrooms, quartered

1 each red and green bell peppers, chopped

1 tbsp (15 mL) dried oregano

1 tsp (5 mL) dried basil

½ cup (125 mL) dry white wine

1 can (28 oz/796 mL) diced tomatoes

1 Sprinkle chicken all over with salt and pepper. In a large shallow Dutch oven, heat half of the oil over medium-high heat and brown chicken on both sides, in batches if necessary. Remove to plate.

2 In the same pot, heat remaining oil over medium-high heat and cook onion, garlic, mushrooms, peppers, oregano and basil for about 15 minutes or until vegetables are beginning to brown, stirring occasionally. Pour in wine and stir vegetables to deglaze pan. Add tomatoes and bring to boil.

3 Return chicken to pot. Reduce heat, and simmer uncovered for about 12 minutes or until chicken is no longer pink inside and sauce is slightly thickened.

CRISPY KOREAN-INSPIRED FRIED CHICKEN STRIPS

SERVES 4

Thanks to the influence of enjoying and cooking different foods at home, Emily's kids have become fond of these fast food-inspired saucy chicken strips.

CHICKEN STRIPS

1 lb (500 g) boneless skinless chicken thighs

1 tbsp (15 mL) sesame oil

1 tbsp (15 mL) minced fresh ginger

$1/2$ tsp (2 mL) each salt and black pepper

$1/4$ cup (60 mL) all-purpose flour

$1/4$ cup (60 mL) cornstarch

1 tsp (5 mL) baking powder

1 tsp (5 mL) garlic powder

Canola oil for frying

SAUCE

$1/4$ cup (60 mL) soy sauce

$1/4$ cup (60 mL) ready-to-use chicken broth

3 tbsp (45 mL) rice vinegar

2 tbsp (30 mL) granulated sugar

1 tbsp (15 mL) cornstarch

2 garlic cloves, minced

1 tsp (5 mL) paprika

1 tsp (5 mL) sesame oil

1 CHICKEN STRIPS: Cut chicken thighs into $1/2$-inch (1 cm) thick strips and place in a bowl. Add sesame oil, ginger, salt and pepper and toss to coat. Let stand for 15 minutes.

2 In a shallow bowl, whisk together flour, cornstarch, baking powder and garlic powder.

3 Meanwhile, in a large heavy pot, heat about 2 inches (5 cm) of oil over medium-high heat to about 350°F (100°C).

4 SAUCE: In a small saucepan, whisk together soy sauce, chicken broth, vinegar, sugar, cornstarch, garlic, paprika and sesame oil. Bring to a simmer, whisking, and remove from heat.

5 CHICKEN STRIPS: In batches, dredge chicken into flour mixture to coat and place carefully into hot oil. Cook, stirring gently, for about 5 minutes or until golden brown and chicken is no longer pink inside. Remove with a slotted spoon into a large bowl. Repeat with remaining chicken.

6 Pour sauce over chicken and toss to coat well.

SPICY VARIATION

For a spicier version of the sauce, substitute 1 tsp (5 mL) gochujang paste for the paprika.

CURRY FRIED CHICKEN WITH HOT HONEY

SERVES 6 TO 8 ·

We love a twist on a classic. The chicken is marinated for the first layer of flavor, tossed in a mild curry coating, then fried until crispy and golden. Enjoy each crunchy bite with a sweet heat drizzle of honey — so delicious!

MARINADE

2 tbsp (30 mL) lime juice

2 tbsp (30 mL) soy sauce

2 green onions, finely chopped

3 garlic cloves, minced

2 tbsp (30 mL) grated fresh ginger

1 tbsp (15 mL) curry powder

1 tbsp (15 mL) packed brown sugar

1 tsp (5 mL) ground cumin

1 tsp (5 mL) chili powder

8 bone-in, skin-on chicken thighs or drumsticks

COATING

1/2 cup (125 mL) all-purpose flour

1/4 cup (60 mL) cornstarch

1 tbsp (15 mL) curry powder

1 tsp (5 mL) salt

1 tsp (5 mL) onion powder

1/2 tsp (2 mL) black pepper

Canola oil

HOT HONEY

1/4 cup (60 mL) liquid honey

2 tsp (10 mL) Sriracha

1 MARINADE: In a large bowl, combine lime juice, soy sauce, green onions, garlic, ginger, curry powder, brown sugar, cumin and chili powder until smooth.

2 Add chicken and stir to coat well. Cover and refrigerate at least 4 hours or overnight.

3 Remove chicken from refrigerator. Preheat oven to 200°F (100°C). Line a baking sheet with paper towels and set a rack on top. In a deep, heavy, wide pot or deep fryer, heat 4 inches (10 cm) of oil over medium-high heat to 350°F (180°C).

4 COATING: Set aside a baking tray. In a shallow bowl, whisk together coating ingredients. Lift one piece of chicken at a time, coat well in flour mixture and place on tray. Repeat with remaining chicken pieces. Discard any remaining marinade and coating.

5 Gently place a few pieces of chicken in oil. Cook for 6 minutes or until starting to turn golden. Gently turn pieces over and cook for about 5 minutes or until golden brown and a meat thermometer inserted in the thickest part of a piece registers 165°F (74°C). Transfer cooked chicken to rack on prepared baking sheet and keep warm in oven. Repeat with remaining chicken pieces.

6 HOT HONEY: In a small bowl, combine honey and Sriracha; drizzle over chicken.

TIP

Swap out the Sriracha with your favorite hot sauce.

CHICKEN FRIED STEAK (WITH CHICKEN) AND MILK GRAVY

SERVES 6 TO 8

There is something unique but familiar about this recipe that keeps the kids (and adults) coming back for more. Any favorite potato side dish would be a perfect match for the chicken and the gravy.

CHICKEN FRIED STEAK

3 boneless skinless chicken breasts (about 1³/₄ lbs/875 g)

¹/₃ cup (75 mL) milk

1 large egg

1 tbsp (15 mL) lemon juice

¹/₂ tsp (2 mL) salt, divided

1 cup (250 mL) all-purpose flour

¹/₂ tsp (2 mL) garlic powder

¹/₄ tsp (1 mL) black pepper

¹/₃ cup (75 mL) canola oil

3 tbsp (45 mL) butter, divided

MILK GRAVY (WHITE GRAVY)

2 tbsp (30 mL) all-purpose flour

2 cups (500 mL) milk

³/₄ tsp (3 mL) each salt

¹/₄ tsp (1 mL) black pepper

1 CHICKEN FRIED STEAK: Using a sharp knife, remove tenderloins and set aside. Cut each chicken breast in half horizontally and if necessary pound each half to make a thin, even piece; set aside.

2 In a shallow bowl, whisk together milk, egg, lemon juice and half of the salt. In another shallow bowl, whisk together flour, garlic powder, remaining salt and pepper.

3 Dip each piece of chicken into milk mixture to coat. Dredge into flour mixture to coat well, shaking off any excess. Repeat with remaining pieces; discard any remaining marinade and flour mixture.

4 In a large nonstick skillet, heat oil and 2 tbsp (30 mL) of the butter over medium-high heat. Fry breaded chicken in batches for about 3 minutes per side or until golden brown. Repeat with remaining chicken. Remove from pan and place on rack on baking sheet; keep warm.

5 MILK GRAVY: Return skillet to medium heat and add remaining butter to melt. Whisk flour into butter. Cook, stirring for about 1 minute or until flour mixture is golden. Slowly whisk in milk and cook, whisking for about 5 minutes or until thickened and bubbly. Stir in salt and pepper. Serve with chicken.

TIP

Chicken Fried Steak is usually made with beef; this is our chicken version.

CHICKEN PARMIGIANA WINGS

SERVES 4 ·

Take these simple breaded wings a step further and create a delicious, finger-licking Parmigiana finger food. The family will love Friday night fun with this favorite.

2 lbs (1 kg) chicken wings, tips removed

3 tbsp (45 mL) canola oil

1/3 cup (75 mL) seasoned dry bread crumbs

1/4 cup (60 mL) grated Parmesan cheese

1 tsp (5 mL) dried Italian seasoning

1/4 tsp (1 mL) each salt and black pepper

1 cup (250 mL) tomato basil pasta sauce

1/2 cup (125 mL) shredded mozzarella cheese

1 Preheat oven to 400°F (200°C). Line a baking sheet with parchment paper.

2 In a large bowl, toss chicken wings with oil to coat. In a small bowl, combine bread crumbs, Parmesan, Italian seasoning, salt and pepper. Sprinkle over chicken and toss to coat evenly.

3 Place chicken wings in a single layer on prepared baking sheet and bake for 25 minutes or until golden brown and no longer pink inside, turning once.

4 Push chicken wings together and spoon sauce over top of wings. Sprinkle with mozzarella cheese and return to oven for 5 minutes or until cheese is melted.

Sylvia and Emily always work in the kitchen together. They are taste buds.

HONEY MUSTARD SPATCHCOCKED CHICKEN

SERVES 5 · · ·

This humble roast chicken is so juicy and flavorful, you're going to want to make two so you have plenty to enjoy the next day. As the chicken is spatchcocked, a fancy term for "split open," it cooks a little faster than a whole bird. The sauce is brushed on the chicken in layers to create a flavorful caramelized glaze.

1/4 cup (60 mL) liquid honey

3 garlic cloves, minced

2 tbsp (30 mL) grainy mustard

1 tbsp (15 mL) Dijon mustard

1 tbsp (15 mL) canola oil

1 1/2 tsp (7 mL) salt

1 tsp (5 mL) paprika

1 whole chicken (3 1/2 to 4 lbs/1.75 to 2 kg)

1 Preheat oven to 425°F (220°C). Set aside a foil lined rimmed baking sheet. In a small bowl, combine honey, garlic, mustards, oil, salt and paprika; set aside.

2 Pat the chicken dry with paper towel. Using a sharp pair of kitchen scissors or a knife, cut along each side of the backbone and remove it. Open the chicken up and turn it over so it is breast side up. Firmly press down on the breastbone until you feel it pop; the chicken should now lie flat. Remove any excess giblets and use in making stock.

3 Place chicken on the prepared baking sheet and brush both sides of the chicken with about 2 tbsp (30 mL) of sauce. Roast chicken for 20 minutes, then brush with 2 tbsp (30 mL) sauce. Roast another 20 minutes, then brush remaining sauce on top. If the skin starts to brown too quickly, loosely tent it with foil. Roast an additional 5 minutes or until the chicken is done. Insert a meat thermometer in the thickest part of the chicken thigh; it should register 165°F (74°C).

4 Remove the chicken from the oven, loosely tent it with foil (if you haven't already) and let rest for 10 minutes before carving. Serve the chicken with the pan juices.

TIP

Any leftover chicken is delicious in a sandwich, casserole, topped on pizza, added to soup or salad.

TURKEY CHILI

SERVES 4 TO 6 · ·

Chili is versatile and can be enjoyed on its own or in other dishes. Make this recipe ahead and freeze in single portions — it's perfect to pack for lunches.

1 lb (500 g) lean ground turkey

1 tbsp (15 mL) canola oil

1 onion, finely chopped

1 green bell pepper, chopped

4 garlic cloves, minced

1 tbsp (15 mL) chili powder

2 tsp (10 mL) dried oregano

1 tsp (5 mL) ground cumin

1 jalapeño pepper, seeded and minced

1 can (28 oz/796 mL) diced tomatoes

1 can (19 oz/540 mL) red kidney beans, drained and rinsed

1/2 cup (125 mL) ready-to-use vegetable or chicken broth

1/4 cup (60 mL) tomato paste

2 bay leaves

1 In a large saucepan, brown turkey, breaking up with spoon. Drain in colander, set aside and return pot to medium heat. Add oil and cook onion, green pepper, garlic, chili powder, oregano and cumin for about 5 minutes or until softened.

2 Return turkey to pan with jalapeño pepper and cook, stirring for 1 minute. Add tomatoes, beans, broth, tomato paste and bay leaves. Bring to a boil; reduce heat, cover slightly and simmer, stirring occasionally for about 20 minutes or until thickened. Remove bay leaves before serving.

TIP

Looking for a spicier chili? Simply add some of your favorite hot sauce to the bowl or add 1/4 tsp (1 mL) cayenne along with the spices when cooking the chili.

Why couldn't the chili practice archery? He didn't hab-en-ero.

TURKEY THIGH CARNITAS

SERVES 8 ·

The slow cooker helps create pieces of tender flavorful turkey perfect for tucking into tortillas. The refreshing bite of mango and cilantro makes these addictive.

4 turkey thighs (about 2½ lbs/1.25 kg)

1 tbsp (15 mL) ancho chili powder

2 tsp (10 mL) ground cumin

2 tsp (10 mL) dried oregano

1 tsp (5 mL) dried thyme

1 tsp (5 mL) smoked paprika

1 tsp (5 mL) salt

3 tbsp (45 mL) canola oil, divided

4 garlic cloves, minced

1 poblano pepper, seeded and thinly sliced

1 small onion, thinly sliced

½ cup (125 mL) orange juice

½ cup (125 mL) barbecue sauce

12 to 16 small corn tortillas, about 1 package (336 g)

1 mango, diced

½ cup (125 mL) chopped fresh cilantro

1 Remove skin from turkey thighs and discard.

2 In a bowl, mix together chili powder, cumin, oregano, thyme, smoked paprika and salt. Rub all over turkey thighs.

3 In a large skillet, heat 2 tbsp (30 mL) of the oil over medium-high heat and brown thighs, in batches if necessary, on both sides.

4 Place in slow cooker. Reduce heat in skillet to medium heat and add remaining oil. Add garlic, poblano and onion and cook for about 5 minutes or until softened. Scrape into slow cooker.

5 Whisk together orange juice and barbecue sauce and pour over top. Cover and cook on Low for 8 hours or on High for 4 hours.

6 Using two forks, shred meat and discard bones. Stir meat into sauce. Divide turkey among tortillas and top with mango and cilantro to serve.

TURKEY BREAST VARIATION

Omit turkey thighs and substitute 2 boneless skinless turkey breasts. You can also use bone-in turkey breasts; simply remove the skin. Once cooked, remove bones from breasts before shredding.

MAKE AHEAD

Make the turkey carnita mixture ahead; cover and refrigerate it for up to 2 days and warm over low heat to enjoy another night. Another option is to freeze the mixture for up to 2 weeks.

TURKEY SLIDERS WITH PEACHES AND BRIE

SERVES 12 ·

These sliders showcase how local fruit and protein
go so well together! Pick ripe but firm peaches
for the best flavor and celebrate summer.

2 ripe but firm peaches,
  quartered

1 tbsp (15 mL) canola oil

1 lb (500 g) ground turkey

2 tbsp (30 mL) chopped
  fresh basil

1 small garlic clove, minced

$1/2$ tsp (2 mL) each salt
  and black pepper

1 small Brie-style cheese
  (4 oz/125 g), cut into
  12 slices

12 slider buns

1 Preheat grill to medium-high heat.

2 In a bowl, toss peach quarters with oil. Place
   on greased grill and grill, turning occasionally,
   for about 6 minutes or until grilled-marked and
   softened. Remove to a cutting board. Reduce grill
   to medium heat.

3 Finely dice enough of the peaches to make $1/2$ cup
   (125 mL). Slice remaining peaches and set aside.

4 In a large bowl, combine turkey, diced peaches,
   basil, garlic, salt and pepper. Shape into 12 small
   patties. Place on grill and cook, turning once, for
   about 10 minutes or until no longer pink inside.
   Place 1 slice of Brie on each patty; close lid and
   let stand on grill for 30 seconds to melt.

5 Serve each patty in a bun and top with remaining
   peach slices.

TIP

Not a Brie fan? No worries; these will be delicious
with any of your favorite cheeses, like sharp (old)
Cheddar, creamy goat cheese or Camembert.
For a real flavor punch, use a creamy blue
cheese instead.

MAKE-AHEAD HERB AND SPICE ROAST TURKEY

SERVES 12 ·

Take the easy way out and roast your turkey a day or two before the big family gathering and then warm it up to enjoy at the table with everyone gathered around. The mixture of spices and herbs makes this turkey sing with flavor.

1/4 cup (60 mL) butter, melted

2 tbsp (30 mL) canola oil

3 tbsp (45 mL) packed light brown sugar

2 tbsp (30 mL) dried sage

1 tbsp (15 mL) dried thyme

1 tbsp (15 mL) ancho chili powder

1 tbsp (15 mL) salt

1/2 tsp (2 mL) black pepper

1/2 tsp (2 mL) garlic powder

1 turkey, giblets and neck removed (about 14 lbs/6.4 kg)

2 celery stalks, coarsely chopped

1 large carrot, coarsely chopped

1 onion, chopped

1 bunch fresh sage

1 cup (250 mL) ready-to-use vegetable or chicken broth

1 Preheat oven to 325°F (160°C).

2 In a small bowl, stir together butter, oil, sugar, sage, thyme, chili powder, salt, pepper and garlic powder.

3 Place turkey on a rack in a roasting pan. Fill back and neck cavity with celery, carrot, onion and sage. Brush all over with spice mixture.

4 Place turkey in oven and roast for about 3 1/2 hours or until thermometer reaches 170°F (77°C). Let turkey rest, covered, for 20 minutes before carving.

5 Carve turkey by removing the legs and thighs. Separate the drumstick and thighs; arrange along the sides of a clean roasting pan. Remove and slice the breast meat, arranging in a shallow layer along the center of the roasting pan. Remove the wings and arrange in the pan. Cover and transfer promptly to the refrigerator overnight.

6 Before reheating, drizzle broth over the breast meat only. Reheat, covered, in 325°F (160°C) oven for about 20 minutes or until warmed through. Transfer to a warm platter.

BBQ VARIATION

If using a barbecue, set soaked wood chips over high on grill. Turn other side of barbecue off and place turkey on unlit side. Try to keep the temperature at 325°F (160°C) in the barbecue while cooking the turkey.

PORK AND LAMB

LEMONGRASS PORK MEATBALLS WITH DIPPING SAUCE

MAKES ABOUT 20 MEATBALLS · ·

These meatballs and dipping sauce are inspired by a traditional Vietnamese dish called Bun Cha. Now we can enjoy its fantastic flavors at home. Use whole lemongrass or choose the convenient pre-chopped lemongrass paste available in a tube or frozen. Enjoy these meatballs and the sweet, savory dipping sauce with rice noodles or in a crusty bun. Be sure to serve with shredded carrots and cucumber, lettuce, cilantro, mint leaves and peanuts.

SAUCE

2 tbsp (30 mL) fish sauce

2 tbsp (30 mL) water

2 tbsp (30 mL) granulated sugar

1 tbsp (15 mL) lime juice

1/4 tsp (1 mL) hot pepper flakes

2 garlic cloves, minced

MEATBALLS

1 lb (500 g) lean ground pork

2 tbsp (30 mL) finely chopped lemongrass or lemongrass paste

3 garlic cloves, minced

1 green onion, finely chopped

2 tsp (10 mL) fish sauce

2 tsp (10 mL) granulated sugar

1/2 tsp (2 mL) cornstarch

1/4 tsp (1 mL) white pepper

Canola oil for frying

1 SAUCE: In a small bowl, combine sauce ingredients; let sit for 10 minutes. Add more water or fish sauce to taste.

2 MEATBALLS: In a medium bowl, add pork, lemongrass, garlic, green onion, fish sauce, sugar, cornstarch and pepper; gently mix until well combined. Refrigerate for 10 minutes to allow the flavors to develop and for the mixture to firm.

3 After the meat mixture has rested, use a small ice cream scoop or 2-tbsp (30 mL) measure to roll mixture into meatballs. In a skillet, heat a little oil over medium-high heat. Add meatballs, working in batches; cook on all sides until browned and meatballs are cooked through, about 10 minutes. Serve with dipping sauce.

TIPS

To use fresh lemongrass, use the white bulb portion (about 6 inches/15 cm). Cut off the tough root end and remove a few of the tough outer layers. Lightly smash lemongrass with the flat part of a knife or with a rolling pin, then finely chop.

White pepper has a more earthy, complex flavor than black pepper.

PORK TENDERLOIN WITH SAGE PESTO

SERVES 5 ·

Flavor-packed sage pesto and pork taste wonderful together. We start by searing the pork on the stove and finish cooking it in the oven for even juicy doneness. Serve this with potatoes or rice and your favorite vegetables.

PESTO

1¾ cups (425 mL) fresh sage leaves, lightly packed

¾ cup (175 mL) fresh parsley, lightly packed

3 garlic cloves

⅓ cup (75 mL) grated Parmesan cheese

¼ cup (60 mL) pine nuts, walnuts or pumpkin seeds

1 tbsp (15 mL) lemon juice

½ tsp (2 mL) each salt and black pepper

½ cup (125 mL) extra virgin olive oil

PORK

2 pork tenderloins (each about 1 lb/500g)

1 tsp (5 mL) paprika

1 tsp (5 mL) salt

½ tsp (2 mL) black pepper

1 tsp (5 mL) canola oil

Lemon wedges

1 PESTO: In the bowl of a food processor (or in a blender), add sage, parsley, garlic, Parmesan, pine nuts, lemon juice, salt and pepper. Pulse a few times until coarsely chopped. In a steady stream, slowly add the olive oil while the food processor is running. Stop to scrape down the sides once or twice. Pulse a few times until mixture is blended. Transfer pesto to an airtight container and store in the refrigerate until ready to use.

2 PORK: Preheat oven to 400°F (200°C). Pat pork dry with a paper towel. In a small bowl, mix paprika, salt and pepper; sprinkle over pork and rub into meat. In a large oven-safe skillet, heat oil over medium-high heat. Add pork and sear on all sides, about 5 minutes.

3 Transfer to oven and bake for 12 to 18 minutes, or until an instant-read thermometer inserted in the thickest part of each tenderloin registers 145°F (63°C).

4 Transfer pork to a cutting board; let rest 5 minutes before slicing into 1-inch (2.5 cm) pieces. Serve with sage pesto, lemon wedges and any accumulated pan juices.

TIPS

Purchase 2 tenderloins that are roughly even in size so they cook evenly.

Any leftover sage pesto is delicious served with simple chicken, mixed into ricotta to spread on crostini, or added to soup, risotto, pasta, or grilled cheese sandwiches.

Pesto freezes well in small jars for up to 3 months. You can also portion it into ice-cube trays; once frozen, transfer to a freezer-safe container.

How do pigs write top-secret messages? With invisible OINK!

BAKED *BLEEPING* ZITI

SERVES 8

Baked pasta is such a heartwarming dinner. Serve it fresh out of the oven with some crusty bread to sop up any sauce that might remain on your plate — classic Italian style, just like the Sopranos.

~~~~~~

1 lb (500 g) boneless pork shoulder, cubed

3/4 tsp (3 mL) salt, divided

1/4 tsp (1 mL) black pepper

1/4 cup (60 mL) extra virgin olive oil (approx.), divided

1 lb (500 g) Italian sausages, cut into 1-inch (2.5 cm) chunks

1/2 cup (125 mL) dry white wine

4 garlic cloves, minced

2 cans (each 28 oz/796 mL) whole tomatoes, with juice

1 cup (250 mL) water

4 large fresh basil leaves

1/4 tsp (1 mL) hot pepper flakes

1 lb (500 g) dried ziti pasta

1 cup (250 mL) shredded mozzarella or provolone cheese, divided

1/2 cup (125 mL) grated Parmesan cheese, divided

1 cup (250 mL) ricotta cheese

1 Sprinkle pork with 1/4 tsp (1 mL) salt and pepper. In a large saucepan, heat 2 tbsp (30 mL) oil over medium-high heat. In batches, add pork and sausages; cook, stirring, about 8 minutes until browned on all sides, adding oil as needed between batches. Using a slotted spoon, transfer meat to a plate. Add wine to the pan, scraping up any browned bits from the bottom. Reduce heat to medium, add garlic and cook, stirring, for 30 seconds. Add tomatoes and water, mashing tomatoes to a coarse texture with a potato masher.

2 Return meat and any accumulated juices to the pan, along with basil, remaining salt and hot pepper flakes. Partially cover and simmer, stirring occasionally for about 2 hours or until pork is falling apart and very tender.

3 Preheat oven to 375°F (190°C). In a large pot of boiling salted water, cook ziti for about 8 minutes or until pasta still has a bite to it. Drain well.

4 Toss ziti with sauce and half each of the mozzarella and Parmesan. Spread half the ziti mixture in a 13- by 9-inch (33 by 23 cm) casserole dish and spoon ricotta over top. Top with remaining ziti mixture and sprinkle with the remaining mozzarella and Parmesan. Cover and bake for 30 minutes. Uncover and bake for 10 minutes or until cheese is melted and edges are bubbly.

GRILLED SAUSAGE PIZZA

SERVES 4 ·

A long oval pizza not only looks cool; it fits on the grill easily.
Make the pizza as an appetizer or for your dinner with
a crisp green salad and enjoy summertime fun.

PIZZA DOUGH

Pinch granulated sugar

²/₃ cup (150 mL) warm
water

2¼ tsp (11 mL) traditional
active dry yeast

2 tbsp (30 mL) extra virgin
olive oil

¼ tsp (1 mL) salt

1½ cups (375 mL)
all-purpose flour
(approx.)

SAUSAGE PIZZA

3 tbsp (45 mL) extra virgin
olive oil, divided

1 small red bell pepper,
quartered

1 yellow summer squash
or zucchini, sliced
lengthwise

1 package (4 oz/125 g)
shiitake mushrooms,
stemmed

2 fresh hot Italian
sausages

⅓ cup (75 mL) pasta
or pizza sauce

1 tbsp (15 mL) store-bought
pesto sauce

1½ cups (375 mL)
shredded mozzarella
or provolone cheese

1 PIZZA DOUGH: In a large bowl, dissolve sugar into water. Sprinkle with yeast and let stand for about 10 minutes or until frothy. Whisk in olive oil and salt. Add flour and scrape out onto floured surface and knead until a soft, smooth dough forms. Cover and let rest on floured surface for 30 minutes.

2 Preheat grill to medium-high heat.

3 SAUSAGE PIZZA: Meanwhile, drizzle half of the oil over red pepper, squash and mushrooms. Place sausages and vegetables on greased grill; close lid and grill, turning frequently, about 5 minutes for mushrooms, 10 minutes for pepper and squash and 15 minutes for the sausages. Remove to bowl; let cool slightly. Slice sausages, pepper, squash and mushrooms; set aside.

4 Cut pizza dough in half and, working on floured surface. push out each half into an oval as thin as desired, to about 12 inches (30 cm) long. Rub remaining oil over both sides of dough and place on greased grill. Grill, turning once, about 5 minutes or until light golden and firm. Remove to cutting board.

5 In a small bowl, combine pasta sauce and pesto. Spread over both pizza doughs. Top each dough with sausage, pepper, squash and mushrooms. Sprinkle with cheese.

6 Reduce the grill heat to low and place pizzas on grill; close lid and grill for about 10 minutes or until cheese is melted and crust is crispy.

OVEN BAKED VARIATION

Instead of grilling pizza, push out dough according to recipe, place on baking sheet and bake in 400°F (200°C) oven for about 20 minutes.

TIPS

Make the pizza dough ahead, place it in an oiled resealable bag and refrigerate it for up to 1 day.

Use leftover grilled vegetables such as eggplant or zucchini as well; any of your favorites will work.

Knock, Knock
Who's there?
Pete.
Pete who?
Pete-za-but you took so long, I've already eaten it!

MUSTARD HERB GRILLED PORK CHOPS

SERVES 6 ·

The mustard and herb marinade ensures juicy and flavorful pork chops. They're simple for a weekday meal, yet special enough to serve to guests. The grilling produces a delicious, caramelized sear on the outside, adding another layer of flavor.

3 tbsp (45 mL) grainy Dijon mustard

3 tbsp (45 mL) soy sauce

2 tbsp (30 mL) liquid honey

1 tbsp (15 mL) cider vinegar

1 tbsp (15 mL) canola oil

1 tbsp (15 mL) chopped fresh rosemary

2 garlic cloves, minced

2 tsp (10 mL) chopped fresh thyme

1 tsp (5 mL) black pepper

6 bone-in pork rib chops, about 1 inch (2.5 cm) thick

1 In a large resealable plastic bag, add mustard, soy sauce, honey, vinegar, oil, rosemary, garlic, thyme and pepper; massage to combine.

2 Add pork chops, seal bag and massage to fully coat. Refrigerate for at least 4 hours or overnight. Remove pork chops from the refrigerator 30 minutes before cooking.

3 Preheat barbecue grill to medium-high. Remove pork from marinade, discarding marinade. Reduce heat to medium; place pork on oiled grill racks. Grill for 5 minutes per side, or until an inserted meat thermometer registers 145°F (63°C) or to desired doneness. Transfer to a serving platter and let rest 5 minutes before serving.

TIP

Look for chops that are the same thickness to ensure even cooking

QUICK BRINE PORK CHOPS

SERVES 4 ·

With these pork chops, you can easily use a brine for
a shorter time to get that juicy end result you are looking for.
Grab a drink and sit back in your lounge chair while the spices,
salt and sugar do their job and you reap the rewards.

2 cups (500 mL) water

3 tbsp (45 mL) kosher salt

2 tbsp (30 mL) maple syrup
or light brown sugar

2 sprigs fresh thyme

1 strip (about
2 inches/5 cm) lemon zest

1 garlic clove, crushed
(optional)

1 tbsp (15 mL) peppercorns

2 cups (500 mL) ice-cold
water

4 bone-in pork loin chops
(about 3/4 inch/2 cm
thick)

1 In a saucepan, over medium-high heat, bring water,
salt and maple syrup to simmer until salt is dissolved.
Remove from heat and add thyme, lemon, garlic and
peppercorns. Stir in ice-cold water and let stand
until room temperature.

2 Place pork chops in a large shallow glass dish. Pour
brine over top of pork chops, making sure chops
are submerged. (Add more cold water if necessary.)
Cover and refrigerate for at least 30 minutes or
up to 4 hours.

3 Remove pork chops from brine and pat dry. Discard
brine. Preheat grill to medium-high heat.

4 Place on greased grill for about 15 minutes, or
until hint of pink remains, turning once. Grill until
an inserted meat thermometer registers 145°F
(63°C) or to desired doneness. Let stand 2 minutes
before serving.

PANFRY VARIATION

Use 1 tbsp (15 mL) of canola oil in a large skillet
and heat over medium-high heat. Cook pork
chops until golden brown and hint of pink remains,
turning once.

TIP

Don't forget to finish grilling your pork chops with
your favorite barbecue sauce.

LAMB AND PISTACHIO MEATBALLS WITH YOGURT MINT SAUCE

MAKES ABOUT 26 MEATBALLS ·

This delicious and flavorful combination of spices and the yogurt sauce were inspired by Middle Eastern cooking. The finishing touch of pistachios adds a wonderful texture to this dish. Serve with a salad and flatbread or rice.

YOGURT MINT SAUCE

½ cup (125 mL) plain Greek-style yogurt

2 tbsp (30 mL) chopped fresh mint

2 tsp (10 mL) mayonnaise

1 tsp (5 mL) lemon juice

1 garlic clove, minced

LAMB MEATBALLS

½ cup (125 mL) dry bread crumbs

½ cup (125 mL) shelled chopped pistachios, divided

2 tsp (10 mL) ground cumin

1 tsp (5 mL) each ground coriander and onion powder

½ tsp (2 mL) each garlic powder and ground cinnamon

½ tsp (2 mL) each salt and black pepper

1 lb (500 g) lean ground lamb

1 large egg, lightly beaten

2 tbsp (30 mL) milk

1 SAUCE: In a small bowl, combine sauce ingredients. Season to taste with salt and pepper. Cover and refrigerate until ready to use.

2 MEATBALLS: Preheat oven to 400°F (200°C); set aside a foil lined baking sheet. In a medium bowl, combine bread crumbs, ¼ cup (60 mL) pistachios, cumin, coriander, onion powder, garlic powder, cinnamon, salt and pepper; stir until combined. Add lamb, egg and milk; mix gently until well combined.

3 Using a small ice cream scoop or 2-tbsp (30 mL) measure, roll mixture into meatballs. Place on prepared baking sheet and bake for 20 minutes or until cooked through. To serve, drizzle with some of the yogurt sauce and sprinkle remaining pistachios on top.

TIPS

Cooked meatballs can be refrigerated for 3 days or frozen for up to 1 month.

You can also enjoy these meatballs tucked into a soft tortilla along with shredded lettuce and sliced tomatoes.

INSTANT POT HERB LAMB STEW

SERVES 8 · 🍲 · 🌾

This mouth-watering stew, rich with tender pieces of fragrant lamb and plenty of vegetables, can feed a crowd. It's a favorite with Sylvia's husband, who enjoys the rich flavor of lamb. The Instant Pot helps speed up the cooking time compared to a stovetop method. The hearty stew tastes even better the next day, so feel free to make this a day ahead.

2 tbsp (30 mL) canola oil

1 large onion, chopped

2 lb (1 kg) boneless lamb, cut into 1-inch (2.5 cm) cubes

1 tsp (5 mL) each salt and black pepper

5 carrots, chopped

3 celery stalks, chopped

1 can (28 oz/796 mL) diced tomatoes

4 garlic cloves, minced

2 tsp (10 mL) dried rosemary

2 tsp (10 mL) dried thyme

1 tsp (5 mL) dried oregano

1 tsp (5 mL) fennel seeds

1 cup (250 mL) ready-to-use chicken broth

3 tbsp (45 mL) water

2 tbsp (30 mL) cornstarch

1 In a 6-quart Instant Pot, select Sauté. Add oil and onion; cook 5 minutes, stirring occasionally. Pat lamb dry with a paper towel then sprinkle with salt and pepper. Add to pot and sauté 5 minutes, stirring occasionally. Add carrots and celery, tomatoes, garlic, rosemary, thyme, oregano, fennel seeds and broth; stir to combine.

2 Press Cancel and lock lid; set pressure release valve to Sealing. Press Manual Pressure Cook; set to High for 25 minutes. (It takes about 10 minutes to come to pressure.)

3 When cooking finishes; let the pressure release naturally for 20 minutes, then release any remaining steam by moving the pressure release valve to Venting. Press Cancel; open lid.

4 Select Sauté. In a small bowl, combine water and cornstarch; stir into stew. Bring to a simmer, stir and cook until stew thickens slightly, about 3 minutes. Press Cancel.

TIPS

Lamb leg or shoulder work equally well in this recipe.

Swap out the carrots and use parsnips or rutabaga.

SERRANO AND SPINACH-STUFFED LEG OF LAMB

SERVES 10 ·

Change up your roast and enjoy some lamb inspired by the flavors of Spain. When you can't take your family to Spain to celebrate, bring a little bit to them.

6 cups (1.5 L) baby spinach

2 tbsp (30 mL) canola oil

1 onion, chopped

3 garlic cloves, minced

2 tsp (10 mL) chopped fresh thyme

2 tsp (10 mL) chopped fresh mint

1/2 cup (125 mL) shredded Manchego cheese

1/3 cup (75 mL) seasoned dry bread crumbs

1/4 cup (60 mL) chopped sun-dried tomatoes in oil, drained

3 tbsp (45 mL) chopped fresh dill

1/4 tsp (1 mL) each salt and black pepper, divided

1 boneless butterflied leg of lamb (about 3 lb/1.5 kg)

4 slices Serrano ham or prosciutto

1 In a large nonstick skillet, cook spinach over medium-high heat for about 3 minutes or until wilted. Drain well and squeeze out liquid. Chop coarsely and place in a bowl; set aside.

2 Return skillet to medium heat. Add oil, onion, garlic, thyme and mint. Cook, stirring for about 4 minutes or until softened. Stir into spinach mixture and let cool slightly. Stir in cheese, bread crumbs, sun-dried tomatoes, dill and half each of the salt and pepper; set aside.

3 Place lamb leg fat side down on surface and lay Serrano ham over top. Spread with spinach mixture, leaving a 1-inch (2.5 cm) border all around. Starting at narrow end, roll up jelly roll style.

4 Tie roast with kitchen string at 1-inch (2.5 cm) intervals. Sprinkle with remaining salt and pepper. Prepare a gas grill for indirect heat: Turn all burners to medium-high heat and close lid. When temperature reaches 325°F to 350°F (160°C to 180°C), turn off one of the burners, creating an indirect heat area, and adjust burners to maintain temperature.

5 Brown lamb on lit side of grill on all sides, then place lamb on unlit side of grill for about 45 minutes. Turn lamb leg once halfway through, and remove from heat once meat thermometer registers 140°F (60°C) for rare. Transfer to cutting board and let rest for about 10 minutes before slicing.

OVEN ROASTING VARIATION
Roast lamb in 350°F (180°C) oven for about 1 1/2 hours.

FISH AND SEAFOOD

HARISSA SHEET-PAN SALMON WITH BROCCOLI AND TOMATOES

SERVES 4 ·

A sheet-pan dinner is always welcome in our kitchen. There's minimal cleanup, perfect for a weeknight meal. The vegetables get a head start on cooking, then the salmon is added midway and baked with a harissa sauce. Harissa is a smoky hot chili pepper paste that provides a flavor punch.

4 cups (1 L) chopped broccoli

2 cups (500 mL) grape tomatoes

1 small onion, sliced

1 tbsp (15 mL) canola oil

1/4 tsp (1 mL) each salt and black pepper

SALMON

4 salmon fillets (about 6 oz/175 g each)

2 tbsp (30 mL) mayonnaise

1 1/2 tbsp (22 mL) harissa paste

2 tsp (10 mL) lemon juice

1 tsp (5 mL) liquid honey

1 tsp (5 mL) soy sauce

1 Preheat oven to 425°F (220°C). Line a rimmed baking sheet with parchment paper or foil.

2 Place broccoli, tomatoes and onion on prepared baking sheet. Add oil, salt and pepper; toss to evenly coat. Spread vegetables out in a single layer and roast 20 minutes, until broccoli is tender crisp.

3 SALMON: Meanwhile, pat salmon dry with paper towels. In a small bowl, combine mayonnaise, harissa, lemon juice, honey and soy sauce. Remove sheet from oven and push vegetables over to one side. Place salmon on baking sheet, skin side down, then brush top and sides with harissa mixture. Drizzle any extra harissa mixture over top vegetables. Return to oven and bake 8 to 10 minutes or until fish flakes when tested.

TIP
Both the broccoli florets and stems can be used in this dish

GRILLED PLANK SALMON WITH MISO BUTTER

SERVES 6 ·

The smoky flavor of the cedar combined with the subtle miso butter is delicious. We love this technique of grilling salmon on a plank — the fish doesn't stick to the grill, plus it makes for easier cleanup and serving. Soaking the plank helps to add flavor as the fish cooks and reduces the risk of the plank lighting on fire.

1 or 2 food-safe cedar planks to fit salmon

6 salmon fillets (about 6 oz/175 g each)

3 tbsp (45 mL) white or yellow miso paste

2 tbsp (30 mL) butter, softened

2 tsp (10 mL) granulated sugar

2 tsp (10 mL) soy sauce

1 tsp (5 mL) toasted sesame seeds

1 green onion, thinly sliced

1 Soak plank in water 1 hour. Remove from water and drain.

2 Preheat barbecue grill to medium-high.

3 Pat salmon fillets dry with paper towel and place skin side down in a single layer on the plank.

4 In a small bowl, stir together miso, butter, sugar and soy sauce. Spread miso mixture over the top and sides of each piece.

5 Place the planked salmon on barbecue, reduce heat to medium and close lid. Grill for 10 to 12 minutes until just opaque throughout and fish flakes easily when tested. Garnish with sesame seeds and green onion.

TIP

White or yellow miso, also known as shiro miso, is mild in flavor. You can use it to add flavor to soups, stocks and salad dressing.

HORSERADISH SALMON BURGERS

SERVES 4 · 🔪 · 🍲

Adding horseradish to canned salmon makes these burgers extra delicious. They're easy to enjoy on their own or tucked into a soft brioche bun with lettuce and tomato.

SALMON BURGERS

2 cans (7 oz/213 g each) salmon, drained

2 large eggs

2 tbsp (30 mL) creamed horseradish

1 tbsp (15 mL) chopped fresh dill

2 tsp (10 mL) minced capers

½ tsp (2 mL) each salt and black pepper

1 cup (250 mL) panko bread crumbs, divided

¼ cup (60 mL) canola oil

DILL PICKLE MAYONNAISE

⅓ cup (75 mL) mayonnaise

1 small dill pickle, finely chopped

1 tbsp (15 mL) pickle juice (optional)

1 tbsp (15 mL) chopped fresh dill

Pinch each salt and black pepper

1 SALMON BURGERS: Scrape salmon and bones into a bowl. Using a fork, mash bones into salmon. Stir in eggs, horseradish, dill, capers, salt and pepper with ¾ cup (175 mL) of the bread crumbs. Mix together and test mixture to make sure it sticks together; if not, sprinkle in a few more bread crumbs if necessary.

2 Divide salmon mixture into 4 patties and place on a large plate. Cover with plastic wrap and refrigerate for at least 1 hour or up to 8 hours.

3 DILL PICKLE MAYONNAISE: In a small bowl, stir together mayonnaise, pickle, pickle juice, if using, dill, salt and pepper; set aside.

4 Place remaining bread crumbs in a shallow dish and coat salmon burgers with bread crumbs.

5 In a large nonstick skillet, heat oil over medium heat and cook for 3 minutes per side or until golden brown. Dollop with Dill Pickle Mayonnaise to serve.

TIP

Use a large flipper to turn the burgers to prevent breakage.

GRILLED JERK FISH SKEWERS

SERVES 5 · 30 ·

These super tasty skewers cook in a flash, especially with the convenience of bottled jerk seasoning paste. Fish varieties such as tilapia, cod, sea bass, halibut and haddock will work well in this recipe. It's perfect for a backyard get together, so double the recipe if you're feeding a crowd.

2 tbsp (30 mL) canola oil

3 tbsp (45 mL) lime juice

2½ tbsp (37 mL) jerk seasoning paste

2 tbsp (30 mL) packed brown sugar

2 tsp (10 mL) soy sauce

1½ lb (750 g) firm white fish

½ fresh pineapple, cut into 1-inch (2.5 cm) cubes (about 3 cups/750 mL)

½ red onion, cut into 1-inch (2.5 cm) squares

1 red bell pepper, cut into 1-inch (2.5 cm) squares

1 green bell pepper, cut into 1-inch (2.5 cm) squares

2 tbsp (30 mL) chopped fresh cilantro

Lime wedges

1 In a medium bowl, combine oil, lime juice, jerk paste, sugar and soy sauce; remove 2 tbsp (30 mL) of mixture for later. Cut fish into 1-inch (2.5 cm) cubes, and pat dry with paper towel. Add fish to jerk mixture; stir to coat well.

2 Meanwhile, preheat barbecue grill to medium-high. Thread the fish, pineapple and vegetables onto skewers, alternating the ingredients. Brush skewers with reserved marinade on both sides. Place skewers on a greased grill for 3 to 4 minutes per side until skewers begin to char and fish is opaque and cooked through.

3 Serve with lime wedges and a sprinkle of cilantro.

TIP

If using bamboo skewers, soak in water for 30 minutes before using.

NOODLE STIR-FRY WITH SHRIMP

SERVES 4 ·

Our good friend Jessie Cayabo says her mom
always serves up a similar style Filipino dish with a splash
of lime juice and fish sauce added at the end. Try it — you
might just become a fan too, as we did.

8 oz (250 g) thin rice
vermicelli noodles

1 lb (500 g) large raw
shrimp, peeled and
deveined

Pinch each salt and black
pepper

2 tbsp (30 mL) canola oil,
divided

1 small onion, thinly sliced

1 carrot, halved and thinly
sliced

1 celery stalk, thinly sliced

4 garlic cloves, minced

3 cups (750 mL) coleslaw
mix or shredded cabbage

1/2 cup (125 mL) ready-
to-use vegetable or
chicken broth

3 tbsp (45 mL) soy sauce

2 tbsp (30 mL) oyster
sauce

1 Place noodles in a large bowl and cover with hot
water; set aside.

2 Toss shrimp with salt and pepper. In a large nonstick
skillet, heat 1 tbsp (15 mL) of the oil over medium-high
heat and sauté shrimp for 3 minutes or until cooked
through; remove to a plate.

3 Drain noodles. Return skillet to medium heat and
add remaining oil. Cook onion, carrot and celery
for about 5 minutes or until softened. Add garlic
and cook, stirring for 1 minute. Increase heat to
medium-high and add coleslaw, broth, soy sauce
and oyster sauce, stirring to combine.

4 Add drained noodles and cook, stirring until noodles
are well coated and liquid is absorbed. Add shrimp
and stir until heated through to serve.

BAKED COCONUT SHRIMP WITH MANGO SLAW

SERVES 6 · 🔲 · 🔪

Sweet, crispy shrimp on top of a fresh bright coleslaw are a delicious combination. The shrimp is coated in a mix of spices and a surprise ingredient — apricot jam — then dipped in coconut and panko for extra crunch. This recipe tastes like summer!

MANGO COLESLAW

4 cups (1 L) thinly sliced green cabbage

1 cup (250 mL) thinly sliced red cabbage

1 carrot, grated

1 green onion, thinly sliced

1 mango, peeled and diced

1/4 cup (60 mL) mayonnaise

3 tbsp (45 mL) cider vinegar

1 tbsp (15 mL) granulated sugar

1 tbsp (15 mL) canola oil

1/2 tsp (2 mL) hot pepper flakes

1/2 tsp (2 mL) salt

SHRIMP

1 1/2 lbs (750 g) large raw shrimp, peeled and deveined

1/4 cup (60 mL) apricot jam

1 tsp (5 mL) salt

1 tsp (5 mL) smoked paprika

1 tsp (5 mL) onion powder

1 tsp (5 mL) garlic powder

1 COLESLAW: In a large bowl, combine green cabbage, red cabbage, carrot, green onion and mango; toss to combine. In a small bowl, combine mayonnaise, vinegar, sugar, oil, hot pepper flakes and salt; stir to combine. Pour dressing over slaw; toss to combine. Refrigerate for 1 hour before serving.

2 SHRIMP: Preheat oven to 425°F (220°C). Set aside a parchment paper lined rimmed baking sheet. Pat shrimp dry with a paper towel. In a bowl, combine shrimp, jam, salt, paprika, onion powder, garlic powder and hot pepper flakes; toss to fully coat. Arrange shrimp in a single layer on prepared baking sheet; sprinkle coconut and panko evenly over top, pressing lightly to adhere. Drizzle with oil.

3 Bake for about 6 to 8 minutes, or until shrimp is firm and cooked through. Serve with mango coleslaw and extra lime wedges.

1 tsp (5 mL) hot pepper
flakes

3/4 cup (175 mL) shredded
unsweetened coconut

2 tbsp (30 mL) panko
bread crumbs

2 tbsp (30 mL) canola oil

TIPS

You can use 5 cups (1.25 L) coleslaw mix in place of the green and red cabbage. You can also try other varieties of cabbage such as napa or savoy.

Shrimp are sold by count per pound. The higher the number, the smaller the shrimp. Large shrimp is labeled 31/35, meaning there are 31 to 35 shrimp in each pound. Extra-large shrimp (26/30) will also work in this recipe; however, they will likely be more pricey.

What do shrimp wear in the kitchen?
A-prawns.

THAI COCONUT CURRY SCALLOP LINGUINE

SERVES 4 TO 6 ·

The warm color of the red curry paste suggests the subtle heat that builds as you enjoy this dish. It's a winner for any weeknight. If you are trying Thai curry paste for the first time, begin with the milder version and see what your family thinks. You may be pleasantly surprised at this creamy delight.

1 package (12 oz/350 g) fresh linguine pasta

1 lb (500 g) sea scallops

1/4 tsp (1 mL) each salt and black pepper

1 tbsp (15 mL) canola oil

1 tbsp (15 mL) Thai red curry paste

1/3 cup (75 mL) chopped fresh cilantro

1 can (14 oz/400 mL) coconut milk

1 In a large pot of boiling salted water, cook linguine for about 5 minutes or until al dente. Drain and set aside.

2 Pat scallops dry with a paper towel. Sprinkle scallops with salt and pepper. In large, deep nonstick skillet, heat oil over medium-high heat and brown scallops on both sides. Remove to a plate.

3 Return skillet to medium heat and add curry paste, stirring for 30 seconds. Add cilantro and cook, stirring for 1 minute. Pour in coconut milk and bring to a boil. Gently add scallops into mixture and reduce to a simmer. Cook for 2 minutes.

4 Add linguine into skillet and stir gently to combine and heat through.

VARIATIONS
Substitute 1 lb (500 g) boneless skinless chicken breasts or salmon, chopped, for scallops. Simmer in coconut milk for about 10 minutes or until cooked through.

TIP
For a bit more curry zip, you can increase the curry paste or double up for a big flavor boost.

GRILLED SHRIMP SOUVLAKI

SERVES 6 ·

Get ready for a mouth-watering meal. We've layered
so much flavor into this grilled dish. Start by marinating the
shrimp. Once grilled, drizzle the shrimp with tzatziki,
then load on the toppings with a side of pita bread.

TZATZIKI

1/2 English cucumber,
  grated

1 cup (250 mL) plain
  Greek yogurt

1 tbsp (15 mL) lemon juice

1 tsp (5 mL) dried dill

1 tsp (5 mL) olive oil

1 garlic clove, minced

Pinch granulated sugar

Salt and black pepper
  to taste

SHRIMP

1 1/2 lbs (750 g) large
  raw shrimp, shelled and
  deveined

1 small red onion, cut into
  1-inch (2.5 cm) squares

3 tbsp (45 mL) canola oil

3 garlic cloves, minced

2 tsp (10 mL) dried oregano

1 tsp (5 mL) dried Italian
  seasoning

1/2 tsp (2 mL) paprika

1/2 tsp (2 mL) each salt and
  black pepper

1 TZATZIKI: Wrap the cucumber in a clean tea towel
  or paper towel and squeeze out excess moisture.
  In a bowl, combine cucumber, yogurt, lemon juice,
  dill, olive oil, garlic and sugar; stir to combine. Add
  salt and pepper to taste. Cover and refrigerate until
  ready to serve.

2 SHRIMP: Pat shrimp dry with paper towel. In a bowl,
  combine shrimp, onion, canola oil, garlic, oregano,
  Italian seasoning, paprika, salt and pepper; toss to
  coat. Refrigerate 30 minutes.

3 Preheat barbecue grill to medium-high. Remove
  shrimp and onions from marinade, discarding
  marinade; thread shrimp and onions onto skewers.
  Reduce heat to medium; place skewers on a
  greased grill for 2 minutes per side or until shrimp
  is cooked through.

4 Serve with tzatziki, pita, lettuce, tomatoes, feta,
  olives and lemon wedges.

6 pita bread

Shredded lettuce

Chopped tomatoes

Crumbled feta cheese

¼ cup (60 mL) sliced olives

Lemon wedges

TIPS

Brush the pita bread with a little olive oil on both sides and heat on the grill if desired.

You can substitute the Greek yogurt with sour cream. The dried dill can be substituted with 1 tbsp (15 mL) fresh dill.

If using wooden skewers, soak for 30 minutes before using.

Why don't shrimp donate to charities?
Because they're shell-fish.

MUSSELS AND BAGUETTE

SERVES 4 ·

A trip to the East Coast is not complete without fresh seafood, and locally harvested mussels are on that list. Whether you use a local wine or beer in your mussels, having a baguette handy to sop up all the juices and broth is essential. Just in case, buy two — trust us!

2 tbsp (30 mL) extra virgin olive oil

1 onion, finely chopped

3 garlic cloves, minced

1/4 cup (60 mL) chopped fresh Italian parsley

1/4 tsp (1 mL) hot pepper flakes

1 cup (250 mL) dry white wine or beer

1/2 cup (125 mL) ready-to-use chicken or fish broth

4 lb (2 kg) mussels, rinsed

2 tbsp (30 mL) butter, softened

2 tbsp (30 mL) all-purpose flour

1 baguette

1 In a Dutch oven or large soup pot, heat oil over medium heat. Add onion, garlic, parsley and hot pepper flakes; cook for about 5 minutes or until softened. Add wine and broth; bring to a simmer. Add mussels, cover and simmer for about 6 minutes or until mussels open.

2 Meanwhile, in a small bowl, mix together butter and flour until smooth.

3 Divide mussels among large, deep bowls. Discard any unopened mussels. Whisk butter mixture into mussel liquid in saucepan and bring to boil. Ladle over top of mussels to serve. Break up baguette and serve with mussels to sop up all the broth.

VEGETARIAN

~

VEGETABLE POT STICKERS

MAKES 50 SMALL POT STICKERS · ·

We love the crispy bottom crust of these pan-fried dumplings. There are many variations in fillings. You don't have to get fancy with the sealing and pleating of the pot stickers; any way you decide, they'll still be delicious. Be sure to cook the pot stickers in a pan that has a tight-fitting lid to hold in the steam. Using convenient store-bought wrappers makes preparing these a little easier. The smaller wrappers create two bite-size pot stickers. Serve with a choice of soy sauce, Sriracha and chili garlic sauce for dipping.

6 dried shiitake mushrooms

Hot water

1 tbsp (15 mL) canola oil

3 cups (750 mL) finely chopped cabbage

1 large carrot, grated

4 green onions, finely chopped

2 garlic cloves, minced

1 tbsp (15 mL) grated fresh ginger

2 tbsp (30 mL) vegetarian oyster sauce

1 tbsp (15 mL) soy sauce

1 tsp (5 mL) sesame oil

50 round dumpling wrappers (about 3 inches/7.5 cm wide)

Canola oil for frying

1 Place mushrooms in bowl, cover with hot water and soak for 30 minutes. Drain, squeeze dry, remove and discard woody stems and finely chop.

2 Line a baking sheet with parchment paper; set aside.

3 In a large skillet, heat 1 tbsp (15 mL) oil over medium-high heat; add mushrooms, cabbage and carrot. Cook, stirring occasionally, for 7 minutes, until vegetables soften. Add green onions, garlic and ginger; cook for 1 minute, until most of the liquid has evaporated. Remove from heat and stir in oyster sauce, soy sauce and sesame oil. Mix until well combined.

4 Place a few wrappers on a clean work surface. (Loosely cover the rest with lightly damp towel to keep them from drying out.) Place a heaping 1 tsp (5 mL) of the filling into the center of each wrapper. Wet the edge of the wrapper with a little water, then fold in a half circle; seal, then pleat if desired. Too much filling will make the wrapper difficult to seal and it might burst during cooking. Place on prepared sheet. Continue until filling and wrappers are used up.

5 In a nonstick pan, over medium-high heat, drizzle a little oil. Working in batches, place pot stickers in pan, seam side up, spacing them about $1/4$ inch (0.5 cm) apart. When the bottom of the pot stickers become golden brown, after about 3 minutes, cover pan. Tilt the lid slightly and add about $1/2$ cup (125 mL) water to the pan and immediately close the lid. (Be careful, as the oil may splatter and plenty of steam is created.) Cook for about 8 minutes, until wrapper is cooked through and liquid has evaporated. Check to see if wrapper edge is tender; add more water and cooking time if necessary. Transfer pot stickers to a serving plate. Repeat with remaining pot stickers, adding more oil to the pan as needed.

MAKE AHEAD

The filling can be made a day ahead. Cover and refrigerate until ready to assemble pot stickers.

Cook only the amount you want to eat. Cover and refrigerate uncooked pot stickers for up to 2 days. Freeze the rest in a single layer on a baking sheet. Once frozen, transfer to a freezer-safe container. Freeze up to 3 months. Cook from frozen as directed, adding a few more minutes to cooking time until filling is heated through.

TIP

Shorter shreds of carrot will make is easier for filling the wrappers.

TOFU LETTUCE WRAPS

SERVES 4 · · · 🌱

This hands-on meal is delicious, a little messy and fun to eat. The beauty of this dish is that each person can customize their wrap with sauce and their favorite toppings.

PEANUT SAUCE

¼ cup (60 mL) hoisin sauce

1 tbsp (15 mL) Sriracha

1 tbsp (15 mL) peanut butter

1 tbsp (15 mL) lime juice

1 tsp (5 mL) sesame oil

1 tsp (5 mL) cider vinegar

½ tsp (2 mL) grated fresh ginger

2 garlic cloves, minced

WRAPS

1 package (12 oz/350 g) extra firm tofu, cut into small cubes

3 tbsp (45 mL) cornstarch

¼ cup (60 mL) canola oil

1 head butter lettuce leaves for wrapping

TOPPINGS

1 carrot, grated

½ red bell pepper, finely diced

2 green onions, sliced

¾ cup (175 mL) roasted peanuts, chopped

Toasted sesame seeds

Hot pepper flakes

1 PEANUT SAUCE: In a small bowl, combine peanut sauce ingredients and blend until smooth; set aside.

2 WRAPS: Wrap tofu in clean tea towel or paper towels and gently press to removed excess water. Place in a bowl and toss with cornstarch to evenly coat. In a skillet, heat half the oil over medium-high heat; add half of the tofu cubes. Fry until gold and crispy on all sides, stirring occasionally, about 5 minutes. Transfer to a plate and repeat with remaining oil and tofu. Transfer second batch to plate.

3 In the same skillet, over medium-high heat, add the peanut sauce and heat for 30 seconds. Remove from heat, gently stir in tofu.

4 To serve, fill lettuce leaves with tofu mixture and garnish with toppings.

TIPS

Other lettuce varieties suitable for wraps include green leaf, romaine or iceberg. Be sure to select a head that is fresh, crisp and hardy enough to hold the filling.

Firm tofu will also work well in this recipe.

Serve with a side of cooked rice or rice noodles if desired.

You can also top your wrap with roughly chopped fresh cilantro (1 cup/250 mL) and serve with lime wedges.

PENNE ALLA VODKA

SERVES 4 · (30) · 🍃

This pasta has a hint of vodka to it, in combination with the tomatoes, which helps keep its creamy texture. If you don't have vodka on hand, dry white wine is a great substitute. This is a big hit with dinner guests and it doesn't take long to make.

1 tbsp (15 mL) butter

1 small onion, finely chopped

1 garlic clove, minced

1/4 cup (60 mL) vodka

1 jar (26 oz/700 mL) strained tomatoes (passata)

1/2 cup (125 mL) heavy or whipping (35%) cream

1 lb (500 g) penne rigate pasta

1/3 cup (75 mL) grated Parmesan cheese

1/4 tsp (1 mL) each salt and black pepper

2 tbsp (30 mL) chopped fresh basil

1 In a skillet, melt butter over medium heat and cook onion and garlic for about 5 minutes or until softened. Add vodka and bring to boil. Add passata and cream; bring to boil and simmer for about 10 minutes or until thickened slightly.

2 Meanwhile, in a large pot of boiling salted water, cook penne for about 10 minutes or until al dente. Drain, reserving some cooking water, and return pasta to pot. Add sauce, Parmesan, salt, pepper and basil; toss to combine, adding a bit of pasta water to moisten if necessary.

KAREN'S TOFU AND GREEN BEANS IN COCONUT CREAM

SERVES 3 TO 4 · · ·

Sylvia's friend Karen Anderson is a food journalist and cookbook author who loves to share her knowledge of food, places to eat and the recipes of friends she's made around the world. This dish is inspired by her frequent trips to South India, where coconut abounds in the lush tropical climate. Serve this dish with roti or naan bread, along with mango chutney.

TOFU

1 lb (500 g) firm tofu, cubed

3 tsp (15 mL) coconut oil, divided

1 garlic clove, minced

1/2 tsp (2 mL) finely chopped jalapeño

1/2 tsp (2 mL) salt

1 tbsp (15 mL) lemon juice

1/2 tsp (2 mL) ground cumin

VEGETABLES AND COCONUT CREAM

3 cups (750 mL) chopped green beans

1 red bell pepper, sliced

1 can (14 oz/398 mL) coconut cream

Pinch ground turmeric

Salt, to taste

1 tbsp (15 mL) finely chopped fresh cilantro

Pinch hot pepper flakes

Mango chutney (optional)

1 TOFU: Pat tofu with a clean tea towel or paper towels to remove excess moisture; set aside.

2 In a medium bowl, add 1 tsp (5 mL) coconut oil, garlic, jalapeño, salt, lemon juice and cumin; stir to combine. Add tofu and gently toss to evenly coat. Marinate 30 to 60 minutes.

3 VEGETABLES AND COCONUT CREAM: In a skillet, heat remaining 2 tsp (10 mL) coconut oil over medium heat; add green beans. Cook, stirring occasionally until tender crisp, about 10 minutes. Add red pepper and cook 3 minutes, or until peppers are tender crisp. Transfer to a plate and set aside.

4 In the same skillet, over medium heat, add coconut cream and turmeric; cook until mixture thickens slightly, about 5 minutes. Add tofu (including marinade), green beans and red pepper; cook until warmed through. Season to taste with salt.

5 Transfer to serving plate and sprinkle with cilantro and hot pepper flakes. Serve with hot cooked basmati rice and chutney, if using.

TIPS

The recipe uses coconut cream, which is richer and thicker than coconut milk.

For a little more heat, increase the amount of jalapeño.

MUSHROOM AND BRIE PUFFED PANCAKE

SERVES 3 TO 4 · ·

This puffed pancake is also known as a Dutch Baby or German pancake. Once removed from the oven, the pancake collapses, creating a perfect edible vessel for the filling. Who wouldn't enjoy gooey melty cheese with savory garlicky mushrooms in a crisp crust? Serve with a side salad or a few handfuls of simple mixed greens on top of the pancake.

PUFF PANCAKE

2 tbsp (30 mL) canola oil

3 large eggs

2/3 cup (150 mL) all-purpose flour

2/3 cup (150 mL) milk

1 1/2 tsp (7 mL) dried thyme

1/2 tsp (2 mL) salt

5 oz (150 g) Brie cheese, cubed

MUSHROOMS

3 tbsp (45 mL) butter

1 lb (500 g) assorted mushrooms, quartered

1/2 tsp (2 mL) each salt and black pepper

3 garlic cloves, minced

1 tsp (5 mL) grainy Dijon mustard

1/2 tsp (2 mL) balsamic vinegar

1 tbsp (15 mL) chopped chives

1 PUFF PANCAKE: Preheat oven to 450°F (230°C). Put oil in a 9- or 10 -inch (23 or 25 cm) cast-iron skillet, swirl to coat the bottom and place in oven as it heats. In a large bowl, whisk eggs, flour, milk, thyme and salt until well combined. Pour mixture into hot skillet. Bake for about 15 minutes or until puffed and golden.

2 MUSHROOMS: Meanwhile, in a skillet, melt butter over medium-high heat. Add mushrooms, salt and pepper and cook for 7 minutes, stirring occasionally, until mushrooms start to brown and most of the liquid has evaporated. Reduce heat to medium, add garlic, mustard and balsamic vinegar and cook another 3 minutes, stirring occasionally. Keep warm until pancake is ready.

3 When pancake is done, remove from oven and top with cheese, warm mushroom mixture and chives. Cut into wedges.

TIP

Keep the oven door closed while the pancake bakes to get maximum puff!

VEGGIE BEAN BURRITOS

SERVES 8 ·

These burritos are perfect to make ahead and
tuck away for lunches or dinners when there's nothing
else around. No one ever seems to miss the meat!

1 tbsp (15 mL) canola oil

1 onion, chopped

4 garlic cloves, minced

1 package (12 oz/340 g)
veggie ground round
(ground soy)

1 tbsp (15 mL) chili powder

1 tsp (5 mL) ground cumin

1/4 tsp (1 mL) each salt
and black pepper

1/4 tsp (1 mL) cayenne

1 can (19 oz/540 mL)
kidney beans, drained
and rinsed

1 cup (250 mL) salsa

8 large flour tortillas (10-
to 12-inch/25 to 30 cm)

2 cups (500 mL) shredded
Cheddar or Monterey
Jack cheese

Sour cream and
guacamole (optional)

1 In a skillet, heat oil over medium heat and cook
onion and garlic for 3 minutes or until softened.
Stir in veggie ground round, chili powder, cumin,
salt, pepper and cayenne; cook, stirring, for about
5 minutes for flavors to develop. Add kidney beans
and stir to combine. Remove from heat and mash
beans into mixture. Stir in salsa.

2 Preheat oven to 350°F (180°C).

3 Lay out tortillas and place about 1/2 cup (125 mL)
of the filling into center of tortilla. Sprinkle with
some cheese. Fold in edges and roll up.

4 Place burritos in a lightly greased casserole dish
or small baking pan. Bake for 20 minutes or until
heated through and lightly golden.

VEGAN VARIATION
Substitute vegan Cheddar shreds for the cheese.

PROTEIN OPTION
Substitute 12 oz (375 g) ground beef, turkey,
chicken or pork for ground soy. Cook first in
skillet until no longer pink inside and drain
before continuing with recipe.

MAKE AHEAD

Wrap tortillas individually in plastic wrap and tuck into resealable freezer bag or container. Freeze for up to 1 month.

TIPS

Want burritos for little hands? Simply use 12 small flour tortillas to wrap up the filling and bake as in recipe.

If frozen, thaw overnight first then cover the burritos when baking in the oven. For a quick warmup, pop the burritos in the microwave.

What do burritos ask when they meet after a long time? "Hey, how you bean?"

GRILLED PANEER KABOBS

SERVES 4 (8 SKEWERS) ·

If you haven't cooked paneer on the grill, this is a great way to try it. Each skewer is filled with veggies and color. A light grilling warms everything up and brings a smoky flavor, adding a nice twist to the lemon curry sauce.

PANEER KABOBS

1 lb (500 g) mini baby potatoes (about 20)

1/4 cup (60 mL) canola oil

3 tbsp (45 mL) lemon juice

1 tbsp (15 mL) chopped chives or green onions

1 tsp (5 mL) chopped fresh tarragon or 1/2 tsp (2 mL) dried

1/4 tsp (1 mL) each salt and black pepper

1 package (12 oz/350 g) paneer

1 large green bell pepper, cubed

1 cup (250 mL) grape tomatoes

LEMON CURRY SAUCE

2 tbsp (30 mL) butter

2 tbsp (30 mL) all-purpose flour

1 cup (250 mL) milk

2 tsp (10 mL) curry paste or powder

1/2 tsp (2 mL) salt

1/2 tsp (2 mL) grated lemon zest

2 tbsp (30 mL) lemon juice

1 **PANEER KABOBS:** In a small pot, boil potatoes for 10 minutes. Drain and let cool.

2 In a large bowl, whisk together oil, lemon juice, chives, tarragon, salt and pepper. Stir in paneer, potatoes, green pepper and tomatoes to coat. Cover and refrigerate for 15 minutes.

3 **LEMON CURRY SAUCE:** Meanwhile, in a saucepan, melt butter over medium heat. Whisk in flour and cook for 1 minute. Gradually whisk in milk until smooth. Cook, stirring frequently for about 4 minutes or until bubbly and thickened. Remove from heat and whisk in curry paste, salt, lemon zest and juice. Keep warm.

4 Preheat grill to medium-high heat. Place potatoes, paneer and vegetables onto skewers, alternating pieces. Grill skewers about 6 minutes, turning occasionally or until cheese is grill-marked.

5 Remove from skewers and spoon Lemon Curry Sauce over top to enjoy.

TIPS

If using wooden or bamboo skewers, be sure to soak them for at least 30 minutes before skewering.

Don't want to skewer? No problem. Sauté all the veggies and paneer in a large skillet until golden brown and then add the sauce to coat. If you are going to use the sauce this way, you may want to double the recipe to ensure everything is well coated.

PEROGIES

SERVES 6 TO 8 (YIELDS ABOUT 3 TO 4 DOZEN PEROGIES) · ·

Sharing family recipes is a time-honored tradition, so when Kate Mlodzik shared her family's recipe for perogies, we were amazed to see how she created a filling for her vegetarian daughter that encompasses tradition with change. Grandma would be proud!

KALE, MUSHROOM AND BEAN FILLING

2 tbsp (30 mL) butter

1 small onion, chopped

1½ cups (375 mL) chopped mushrooms

4 cups (1 L) lightly packed chopped kale leaves

1 cup (250 mL) cooked white kidney beans

½ cup (125 mL) shredded Asiago cheese

½ tsp (2 mL) each salt and black pepper

PEROGY DOUGH

3 cups (750 mL) all-purpose flour (approx.)

1 tsp (5 mL) salt

½ cup (125 mL) whole milk

½ cup (125 mL) water

1 large egg

3 tbsp (45 mL) butter, melted

TOPPING

2 tbsp (30 mL) butter, melted

4 green onions, chopped

Sour cream (optional)

1 KALE, MUSHROOM AND BEAN FILLING: In a large skillet, melt butter over medium heat and cook onion and mushrooms for about 8 minutes or until softened and liquid evaporates. Add kale and beans; cook, stirring about 5 minutes or until kale is wilted. Remove from heat and, using a potato masher, mash mixture well. Stir in cheese, salt and pepper; set aside.

2 PEROGY DOUGH: In a small bowl, whisk together flour and salt. In a large bowl, whisk together milk, water, egg and butter. Add 2 cups (500 mL) of the flour mixture to milk mixture and, using an electric mixer, gently beat in flour. Add remaining flour mixture, stirring with a wooden spoon to combine well. Turn out onto a floured work surface and gently knead dough until soft but not sticky.

3 Cut dough into quarters and roll out to about ¼ inch (5 mm). (Dough should be a bit stretchy.) Using a 3-inch (7.5 cm) cookie cutter, glass or can, cut out circles. Repeat with all the dough. Working in batches helps keep the dough moist. Roll up scraps and reroll as many times as needed to use up the dough. Spoon about 1 tsp (5 mL) of the filling in center of each circle. Stretch dough slightly to close and form a half circle; pinch seam well to seal. Repeat with remaining filling. Place perogies on baking sheet.

4 Bring a pot of salted water to boil. Add perogies and cook for about 10 minutes or until they float to the top. Using a slotted spoon or small sieve, lift perogies out of the water. Cook in batches for best results.

5 TOPPING: Toss with melted butter and serve with green onions and sour cream if using or alternatively heat 1 tbsp (15 mL) canola oil over medium-high heat and pan fry perogies, in batches, to crisp up slightly and serve.

POTATO AND CHEESE FILLING

Boil 1 lb (500 g) peeled yellow-flesh potatoes in salted water until tender. Drain well, mash and set aside. In a skillet, melt 2 tbsp (30 mL) of butter and sauté 1 onion, chopped, for about 5 minutes or until softened. Stir into potatoes along with 1 cup (250 mL) shredded sharp (old) Cheddar cheese and $1/2$ tsp (2 mL) of salt. You should be able to roll mixture into small balls for the filling of the perogies.

SAUERKRAUT AND BACON FILLING

Chop 8 slices of bacon and add to skillet with 2 onions, chopped; cook over medium heat for about 10 minutes until tender and bacon is slightly crispy. Stir in 1 jar (1 L/32 oz) sauerkraut, drained well, and $1/2$ tsp (2 mL) of pepper.

MAKE AHEAD

Uncooked perogies can be made ahead and frozen for up to 2 months.

Once dough is all filled, place baking sheet in freezer and freeze for about 4 hours or until solid. Transfer to resealable bag or freezer container and label.

TIP

If using a 4-inch (10 cm) cutter, you will get fewer perogies, but they will be slightly larger, so more filling can go in.

VEGGIE SAUSAGE CASSOULET

SERVES 4 ·

Everyone in the house will enjoy this one-pot meal. For the best flavor, choose the mild Italian plant-based sausages in the refrigerated or freezer section of the meat department. Use the remaining baguette to sop up all the sauce.

3 tbsp (45 mL) canola oil, divided

1 package (14 oz/400 g) frozen mild Italian plant-based sausages, thawed

1 onion, chopped

1 red bell pepper, chopped

2 cups (500 mL) quartered mushrooms

1 can (19 oz/540 mL) romano beans, drained and rinsed

1½ cups (375 mL) ready-to-use vegetable broth

½ baguette

¼ tsp (1 mL) each salt and black pepper

1 In a large saucepan, heat 1 tbsp (15 mL) of the oil over medium-high heat and brown sausages. Remove to a cutting board and cut into chunks; set aside.

2 Return saucepan to medium heat and add onion, pepper and mushrooms. Sauté for about 5 minutes or until softened. Add sausages, beans and vegetable broth to saucepan. Cover and simmer for 10 minutes. Uncover and simmer for 5 minutes or until thickened slightly.

3 Meanwhile, remove inside crumb from the baguette and break into small bread crumbs. Toss with remaining oil, salt and pepper. Sprinkle over top of cassoulet and broil for about 2 minutes or until golden. Enjoy cassoulet with remaining baguette.

TIPS

For a spicier version, use hot Italian plant-based sausages or add a splash of your favorite hot sauce when serving.

You can substitute white kidney beans or pinto beans for the romano beans.

VEGGIE AND CHEESE LASAGNA

SERVES 8 ·

Some convenience products are meant to be used — like pasta sauce! This lasagna is good for a crowd, so be sure to serve it up on a sports-watching day like Sunday; that's what we do and it's a touchdown every time!

12 dry lasagna noodles

2 tbsp (30 mL) canola oil

1 onion, chopped

1 red bell pepper, chopped

1 small zucchini, chopped

8 oz (250 g) mushrooms, sliced

1 tsp (5 mL) dried Italian seasoning

1/2 tsp (2 mL) each salt and black pepper

1 container (11 oz/312 g) baby spinach

1 tub (16 oz/450 g) ricotta cheese

3 large eggs

1/3 cup (75 mL) grated Parmesan cheese, divided

1 jar (22 oz/650 mL) tomato basil or marinara pasta sauce

1 3/4 cups (425 mL) shredded mozzarella cheese

1 In a large pot of boiling salted water, cook lasagna noodles about 10 minutes or until al dente. Drain and rinse under cold water. Lay noodles flat on damp tea towels; set aside.

2 Meanwhile, in a large nonstick skillet, heat oil over medium-high heat. Cook onion, red pepper, zucchini, mushrooms, Italian seasoning, salt and pepper for about 8 minutes or until golden brown and liquid is evaporated. Add spinach and cook, stirring for about 4 minutes or until wilted.

3 In a bowl, stir together ricotta, eggs and 1/4 cup (60 mL) of the Parmesan cheese; set aside. Preheat oven to 350°F (180°C). Lightly spray a 13- by 9-inch (33 by 23 cm) baking dish with cooking spray.

4 Ladle 1/2 cup (125 mL) of the pasta sauce in bottom of prepared dish. Lay 3 noodles on top of sauce. Spread one third of the ricotta mixture and one third of the spinach mixture. Spread with another 1/2 cup (125 mL) of pasta sauce. Sprinkle with 1/3 cup (75 mL) of the mozzarella cheese. Repeat layers, ending with noodles on top. Spread with remaining sauce and sprinkle with remaining mozzarella and Parmesan cheeses. Cover with foil and bake for 45 minutes. Uncover and bake for 15 minutes or knife inserted in center is hot to the touch. Let cool 10 minutes before cutting and serving.

STORAGE TIP

You can assemble the lasagna and refrigerate it for up to 1 day before baking. Once baked, you can freeze the lasagna whole or in portions. It's great to reheat in the microwave for later lunches.

TIPS

You can substitute oven-ready gluten-free noodles for the regular noodles, which means no boiling the noodles, as they are typically thinner and require no precooking.

You could also substitute fresh lasagna sheets for the dried noodles if you want to reduce some kitchen prep. They do not need to be boiled to use in the recipe.

How do you fix a broken tomato?
With tomato paste.

SIDES

❧

CILANTRO LIME RICE

SERVES 5 TO 6 ·   · ·

A delicious side dish that can also be enjoyed in
a grain bowl or added to a burrito. Long-grain rice
such as basmati or jasmine works well in this recipe.
We like to add a generous helping of cilantro, but feel
free to adjust the amount according to your taste buds.

1½ cups (375 mL) long-grain white rice

2¼ cups (550 mL) ready-to-use vegetable or chicken broth

1 tbsp (15 mL) canola oil

1 tsp (5 mL) salt

½ tsp (2 mL) garlic powder

1 lime, zested and juiced

¾ cup (175 mL) chopped fresh cilantro

1 In a colander, place rice and rinse and drain well. In a medium saucepan, over medium-high heat, combine rice, broth, oil, salt and garlic powder; stir to combine. Bring to a boil, then reduce heat to medium-low, cover and cook 15 minutes.

2 Without lifting lid, turn heat off and let stand 10 minutes. Fluff with a fork and stir in lime juice, zest and cilantro.

TIPS

When chopping cilantro, use the leaves and tender stems.

Refrigerate leftovers for up to 2 days, or freeze for up to 1 month.

OVEN-BAKED FRIED RICE

SERVES 6 ·

We love this take on traditional fried rice. Start with raw rice, toss in the other ingredients, then cover and bake for a fluffy delicious oven dish. The recipe is flexible with the vegetables and meat, making it a perfect way to use whatever you have on hand.

$1^3/_4$ cups (425 mL) long grain white rice

2 cups (500 mL) ready-to-use chicken broth

3 cups (750 mL) diced mixed frozen vegetables

2 tbsp (30 mL) canola oil

2 tbsp (30 mL) soy sauce

1 tbsp (15 mL) hoisin sauce

3 garlic cloves, minced

$1/_2$ tsp (2 mL) black pepper

2 cups (500 mL) cooked diced ham

1 tbsp (15 mL) toasted sesame seeds

2 tsp (10 mL) sesame oil

2 green onions, thinly sliced

Sriracha

1 Preheat oven to 400°F (200°C). In a 13- by 9-inch (33 by 23 cm) baking pan, add rice, broth, vegetables, oil, soy sauce, hoisin sauce, garlic and pepper; stir to combine, then spread into an even layer. Sprinkle ham over top. Cover tightly with foil and bake 40 minutes. Remove foil and bake uncovered for 10 minutes to crisp the ham.

2 Remove from oven and recover with foil; let rest 10 minutes to allow the rice to finish steaming. Remove foil and stir in sesame seeds, sesame oil and green onions. Serve with Sriracha on the side.

TIPS

To make this a meal, serve with fried eggs on top.

You can substitute the ham with cooked chicken, pork or beef.

Use any mix of frozen vegetables; large pieces will need to be diced for even cooking.

AMY'S SLOW COOKER WILD RICE AND BREAD STUFFING

SERVES 12 ·

Amy, who has been friend and colleague with Emily for many years, continues to create wonderful, easy and delicious recipes. We had to share her slow cooker stuffing; it will help keep your kitchen cool during those busy holiday celebrations.

1/4 cup (60 mL) butter, melted

2 onions, finely chopped

2 large celery stalks, finely chopped

4 garlic cloves, minced

2 tbsp (30 mL) crumbled dried sage

1 tsp (5 mL) dried thyme

1 tsp (5 mL) dried rosemary

3/4 tsp (3 mL) each salt and black pepper

2 cups (500 mL) ready-to-use vegetable or chicken broth

1/2 cup (125 mL) wild rice

10 cups (2.5 L) cubed light rye or Calabrese bread (about one 1 1/4 lb/570 g loaf)

1 cup (250 mL) dried cranberries

1/2 cup (125 mL) chopped fresh parsley

1 Stir butter, onions, celery, garlic, sage, thyme, rosemary, salt and pepper together in slow cooker. Cover and cook on High for 30 minutes. Stir in broth and rice and cook on High for 1 hour.

2 Preheat oven to 300°F (150°C). Spread bread cubes on a rimmed baking sheet and bake for 15 minutes, stirring once. Leave on the baking sheet to cool to room temperature.

3 Stir toasted bread cubes, cranberries and parsley into slow cooker until evenly moistened. Reduce heat to Low. Cook, stirring every hour, for 2 1/2 to 3 hours or until stuffing is lightly browned around the edges and the excess moisture is absorbed.

OVEN VARIATION

Melt butter in a large saucepan set over medium heat. Add onions, celery, garlic, sage, thyme, rosemary, salt and pepper; sauté until softened. Add broth and rice. Cover and simmer on low for 35 to 40 minutes or until fluid is mostly absorbed. Cool slightly. Toss the rice mixture with the bread, cranberries and parsley. Transfer to a greased, 13- by 9-inch (33 by 23 cm) baking dish. Cover and bake in a 350°F (180°C) oven for 30 minutes. Uncover and bake an additional 20 minutes or until golden and set.

TIPS

Substitute any crusty whole grain bread for the rye.

You can toast the bread up to 2 days ahead for the stuffing.

HARVEST RISOTTO

SERVES 4 TO 6 · ·

This risotto is perfect to serve alongside your favorite roast but it's also hearty enough to serve on its own or to your favorite vegetarian guest — they will love it and you!

¼ cup (60 mL) extra virgin olive oil, divided

1 shallot, chopped

1½ cups (375 mL) sliced mushrooms

2 garlic cloves, minced

¼ tsp (1 mL) dried rosemary

¼ tsp (1 mL) dried thyme

¼ tsp (1 mL) each salt and black pepper

Pinch hot pepper flakes

1 small zucchini, diced

1 red bell pepper, diced

1 cup (250 mL) corn kernels, optional

1½ cups (375 mL) Arborio rice

½ cup (125 mL) dry white wine

5 cups (1.25 L) ready-to-use vegetable or chicken broth, hot

1 cup (250 mL) fresh grated Parmesan cheese

1 In a large saucepan, heat half of the oil over medium heat; cook shallot, mushrooms, garlic, rosemary, thyme, salt, pepper and hot pepper flakes, stirring often, for about 5 minutes or until softened.

2 Add zucchini, red pepper and corn, if using; cook for 3 to 5 minutes or until softened and any excess liquid has been evaporated. Scrape into a large bowl.

3 Add remaining oil to pan and stir in rice until well coated. Pour in wine and cook, stirring, until all of the wine is absorbed. Add stock, ½ cup (125 mL) at a time, cooking and stirring until each addition is absorbed before adding the next, for about 18 minutes or until rice is tender and creamy.

4 Stir in reserved vegetable mixture and Parmesan until melted. Serve immediately.

BARLEY VARIATION

Omit rice and substitute 1 cup (250 mL) pearl or pot barley and add about 5 minutes to cooking time.

RISOTTO CAKES

Use 3 cups (750 mL) of leftover risotto or make a fresh batch and spread it out onto a baking sheet to cool and use. Stir in ⅓ cup (75 mL) of seasoned dry bread crumbs and ¼ cup (60 mL) grated Parmesan cheese. Shape into 3-inch (8 cm) round patties. In a large nonstick skillet, heat oil over medium-high heat and pan fry, turning once, for about 5 minutes or until golden brown and crisp. If you have some pasta sauce or salsa in the fridge, be sure to warm it up to serve with the risotto cakes to dip into. You won't regret it!

GRILLED POTATOES AND ROASTED GARLIC

SERVES 6 ·

Potatoes can be boring, so we punched them up by grilling the potatoes and adding tons of garlic for an added kick of flavor. This is great to serve with your grilled favorites this summer.

6 yellow-fleshed potatoes, scrubbed

1/3 cup (75 mL) extra virgin olive oil, divided

1/4 cup (60 mL) chopped fresh basil

1 tbsp (15 mL) chopped fresh rosemary

1/2 tsp (2 mL) each salt and black pepper

1 head roasted garlic (see Roasted Garlic tip)

2 tbsp (30 mL) chopped oil packed sun-dried tomatoes, drained

2 tbsp (30 mL) balsamic vinegar

1 tsp (5 mL) Dijon mustard

1 Pierce potatoes all over with fork. Place in microwaveable container with 1/4 cup (60 mL) of water. Cover with plastic wrap. Cook on High for about 12 minutes or until tender. Let cool slightly.

2 Meanwhile, whisk together 3 tbsp (45mL) of the oil, basil, rosemary, salt and pepper. Slice potatoes into thirds. Toss gently with oil mixture. Place on greased grill over medium-high heat for about 10 minutes or until crisp and golden. Remove to platter.

3 Squeeze roasted garlic into a bowl. Whisk in remaining oil, sun-dried tomatoes, vinegar and mustard. Spoon over potatoes to serve.

ROASTED GARLIC

Roasted garlic is a huge flavor boost for so many recipes but also delicious on its own, spread over bread with a drizzle of oil. Be sure to roast multiple heads of garlic and freeze what you don't need for an easy addition to recipes like this one.

Cut top stem end of garlic head off to expose cloves slightly. Place on piece of foil and drizzle with some oil. Wrap well and roast in 400°F (200°C) oven for about 35 minutes or until soft when pressed. Let cool until easy to handle; squeeze out garlic cloves from skin to use. Freeze cooled roasted garlic heads in airtight container or resealable freezer bags for up to 3 months. Thaw or defrost in microwave or oven before using.

STEAMED MINI POTATOES WITH GARLIC HERB BUTTER

MAKES 6 SERVINGS · · ·

For this recipe, we've skipped using a large pot of boiling water to cook potatoes. Try steaming these little potatoes to retain more flavor. The butter is heated for a few minutes until slightly brown, adding a nutty richness to this dish.

2 lbs (1 kg) baby potatoes, halved

2 tbsp (30 mL) butter

2 garlic cloves, minced

1 tbsp (15 mL) finely chopped fresh parsley

1 tbsp (15 mL) finely chopped fresh chives

1 tsp (5 mL) finely chopped fresh thyme

1/2 tsp (2 mL) salt

1/4 tsp (1 mL) black pepper

2 tbsp (30 mL) grated Parmesan cheese

1 In a medium pot, add 1 inch (2.5 cm) water. Place potatoes in a steamer basket, cover pot and steam until potatoes are tender, about 15 minutes. Remove the potatoes; set aside.

2 Drain water from pot and place it back on stove. Add butter, melt it over medium heat for 4 minutes, or until butter sizzles and begins to brown a little. Add garlic and cook 30 seconds, then stir in parsley, chives, thyme, salt, pepper and potatoes; gently toss to evenly coat. Transfer to serving dish and sprinkle with Parmesan.

TIP
Make this vegan by swapping out the butter with vegan butter or vegetable oil and vegan Parmesan cheese for the dairy Parmesan cheese.

SAUTÉED KALE AND MUSHROOMS

SERVES 4 ·

Quick and simple, this sautéed kale combined with buttery sautéed mushrooms is delicious!

2 tbsp (30 mL) butter

8 oz (250 g) sliced mushrooms (about 4 cups/1 L)

1 garlic clove, minced

1 tsp (5 mL) maple syrup or liquid honey

1/2 tsp (2 mL) cider vinegar

1 container (5 oz/142 g) baby kale or baby kale blend

Salt and black pepper, to taste

1 In a large nonstick skillet, melt butter over medium-high heat. Add mushrooms and sauté for 3 minutes. Add garlic, maple syrup and vinegar and sauté 10 seconds, then stir in kale. Reduce heat to medium; cover and cook for 3 minutes until kale is wilted. Season to taste with salt and pepper. Serve immediately.

TIPS

Try these tasty greens tossed with pasta, on top of toasted bread or added to a grain bowl.

Make it vegan by swapping out the butter with vegan butter and using the maple syrup.

How much room is needed for fungi to grow? As mush-room as possible.

SKILLET CABBAGE AND CELERY

SERVES 4 · · · ·

Cabbage and celery dressed up with onions and garlic is a tasty way to enjoy these vegetables. Savoy cabbage has deep green-colored leaves and a crinkly texture. Napa cabbage, also known as Chinese cabbage, has long, light green leaves with thick white stalks. Both varieties have a milder flavor than green cabbage.

1 tsp (5 mL) canola oil

1/2 small onion, thinly sliced

1/2 tsp (2 mL) salt

4 cups (1 L) thinly sliced napa or savoy cabbage

3 celery stalks, thinly sliced

2 garlic cloves, thinly sliced

1 cup (250 mL) ready-to-use vegetable or chicken broth

Black pepper, to taste

1. In a large nonstick skillet, heat oil over medium-high heat. Sauté onion and salt for 2 minutes. Add cabbage, celery, garlic and cook, stirring often for 5 minutes, until beginning to soften.

2. Add broth; reduce heat to medium and simmer for about 10 minutes, stirring occasionally until vegetables are tender. Add pepper to taste.

TIP
If napa or savoy cabbage is not available, use green cabbage and cook until tender.

ZUCCHINI FRITTERS

MAKES ABOUT 16 FRITTERS · ·

Emily's friend Kate's daughter Julia exclaimed that this recipe had turned the inferior zucchini into a tasty vegetable — a perfect compliment from a vegetarian who knows her veggies! Enjoy these on their own or with this little pesto mayo to dip into.

ZUCCHINI FRITTERS

1 cup (250 mL) all-purpose flour

¼ cup (60 mL) grated Parmesan cheese

3 tbsp (45 mL) chopped fresh herbs (such as parsley, mint and basil)

2 tsp (10 mL) baking powder

¾ tsp (3 mL) salt

1 cup (250 mL) sparking water or light beer

¾ cup (175 mL) canola oil (approx.)

1 cup (250 mL) grated zucchini, squeezed, or 12 fresh zucchini flowers, chopped

PESTO MAYO

¼ cup (60 mL) light mayonnaise

4 tsp (20 mL) basil pesto

1 ZUCCHINI FRITTERS: In a bowl, whisk together flour, Parmesan, herbs, baking powder and salt. Pour in water, whisking until consistency of thick pancake batter.

2 Pour enough oil to fill bottom of large nonstick skillet. Heat over medium-high heat.

3 Gently stir zucchini into batter to coat well. Using a spoonful of batter at a time, place into skillet. (Do not crowd the pan.) Let cook for about 3 minutes, until the batter starts to set and almost bubble around the edges. Carefully turn over and cook until light golden brown. Remove to paper towel-lined plate and repeat with remaining batter.

4 PESTO MAYO: In a small bowl, whisk together mayonnaise and pesto. Serve with fritters.

TIPS

Once cooled, refrigerate for up to 2 days. To reheat fritters, place them on a baking sheet in a 350°F (180°C) oven until they are crisp.

Cook them like pancakes and look for those little bubbles to form before turning them to cook the other side.

You will need about 1 medium zucchini to get the 1 cup (250 mL) grated.

ZUCCHINI FLOWER VARIATION

Omit zucchini and, instead of stirring in zucchini flowers, dip each flower into batter and fry as in recipe. Be sure to remove stamen from flowers before using.

SWEETS

~

ZUCCHINI OAT COOKIES

MAKES ABOUT 24 COOKIES ·

These cakey cookies are chock full of chocolate chips and a hint of warm spices in every bite. Quick-cooking oats add a chewy texture and the zucchini helps keep the cookies soft.

1 cup (250 mL) lightly packed grated zucchini, unpeeled

3/4 cup (175 mL) packed dark brown sugar

1/3 cup (75 mL) canola oil

1 large egg, lightly beaten

1 tsp (5 mL) vanilla

1 1/4 cups (300 mL) all-purpose flour

1 cup (250 mL) quick-cooking oats

1 tsp (5 mL) ground cinnamon

1 tsp (5 mL) baking powder

1/2 tsp (2 mL) salt

1/4 tsp (1 mL) baking soda

1/4 tsp (1 mL) ground cloves

1 cup (250 mL) chocolate chips

1 In a large bowl, stir together zucchini, brown sugar, oil, egg and vanilla until combined. In a medium bowl, whisk together flour, oats, cinnamon, baking powder, salt, baking soda and cloves. Stir dry ingredients into zucchini mixture until just combined. Stir in chocolate chips. Let stand at room temperature for 25 minutes to allow the oats to absorb some of the moisture.

2 Preheat oven to 350°F (180°C). Line two baking sheets with parchment paper. Using a small ice-cream scoop or 2 tbsp (30 mL) measure, drop dough onto prepared baking sheets, about 2 inches (5 cm) apart. Bake, one sheet at a time, for 13 to 15 minutes, until golden around the edges and bottoms are beginning to brown. (Do not overbake.) Let cool on baking sheet for 5 minutes, then transfer to a cooling rack.

TIP

Store in an airtight container at room temperature for up to 2 days or freeze for up to 1 month.

BROWNIE COOKIE

MAKES ABOUT 16 COOKIES ·

Change it up and make a batch of these cookies
instead of a pan of brownies. The hint of orange makes
us think of those chocolate orange slices so many
enjoy during the holidays — now enjoy it all year long!

½ cup (125 mL) butter

5 oz (150 g) chopped
semisweet or bittersweet
chocolate

⅔ cup (150 mL) packed
light brown sugar

1 tsp (5 mL) vanilla

½ tsp (2 mL) grated
orange zest

2 large eggs

1¼ cups (300 mL)
all-purpose flour

Pinch salt

1 In a saucepan, combine butter, chocolate and
brown sugar and melt over low heat until smooth
and combined. Whisk in vanilla and orange zest.
Let cool slightly.

2 Whisk in eggs, one at a time, whisking well after
each addition. Add flour and salt; stir well until
combined.

3 Preheat oven to 350°F (180°C). Line a baking sheet
with parchment paper.

4 Using a mini ice-cream scoop, or heaping
tablespoon (15 mL), scoop out mixture onto prepared
pan. Bake for about 8 minutes or until top is just set.
Let cool on pan on rack.

**Why did the boy put a candy bar under his pillow?
So he would have sweet dreams.**

BLACK FOREST FLOURLESS MINI CAKES

SERVES 10 ·

These fudgy individual desserts make it easy to serve to family and guests, which makes them perfect for relaxed entertaining. The mini cakes puff up during baking, fall when cooled, leaving the perfect shape to fill with whipped cream and kirsch-laced cherry sauce.

6 oz (175 g) semisweet or dark chocolate, chopped

1/2 cup (125 mL) butter

6 large eggs

3/4 cup (175 mL) granulated sugar

1/2 cup (125 mL) unsweetened cocoa powder

1/4 tsp (1 mL) salt

CHERRY SAUCE

4 cups (1 L) frozen pitted sweet cherries, halved and thawed

2 tbsp (30 mL) granulated sugar

2 tbsp (30 mL) water

1 tbsp (15 mL) cornstarch

1/8 tsp (0.5 mL) salt

1 to 2 tbsp (15 to 30 mL) kirsch (cherry brandy)

1 cup (250 mL) heavy or whipping (35%) cream

Unsweetened cocoa powder

1 Preheat oven to 350°F (180°C). Place ten 1/2-cup (125 mL) oven-safe lightly greased ramekins on a baking tray; set aside.

2 In a medium bowl set over a pot of barely simmering water, gently melt chocolate and butter; stir occasionally until smooth.

3 Meanwhile, in a stand mixer, using whisk attachment, beat eggs and sugar at high speed for 2 minutes, until mixture is light in color. Sift in cocoa and salt, then add cooled chocolate mixture and mix just until combined. Evenly divide the batter into the ramekins. Bake for 15 to 18 minutes, until tops are puffed; center should still be slightly jiggly. Cool on a wire rack; centers will sink.

4 CHERRY SAUCE: In a pot, over medium heat, add cherries (and any accumulated juices) and sugar; bring to a gentle boil. Reduce the heat to low and simmer for 3 minutes. In a small bowl, combine water and cornstarch and stir into the cherries; add salt. Cook 2 minutes, stirring occasionally. Remove from heat, let cool slightly and stir in kirsch.

5 In a bowl, using an electric mixer, whip cream to soft peaks. When ready to serve, top each cake with a dollop of whipped cream, a spoonful of cherry sauce and a dusting of cocoa powder.

MAKE AHEAD

Cakes can be refrigerated for up to 3 days or frozen for up to 2 months.

DAIRY-FREE CHOCOLATE GINGER SNACK CAKE

SERVES 9 ·

With a deep chocolate flavor paired with ginger, this moist cake is delicious as a snack and fancy enough for dessert. Candied ginger on top makes it extra special.

CAKE

1 cup (250 mL) all-purpose flour

3/4 cup (175 mL) unsweetened cocoa powder

1/2 tsp (2 mL) each salt and baking powder

1/4 tsp (1 mL) baking soda

1/4 tsp (1 mL) ground ginger

3/4 cup (175 mL) oat milk

2 large eggs

3/4 cup (175 mL) packed brown sugar

2/3 cup (150 mL) canola oil

2 tsp (10 mL) finely grated fresh ginger

1 tsp (5 mL) vanilla

ICING

1 cup (250 mL) confectioners' (icing) sugar

1/4 cup (60 mL) unsweetened cocoa powder

3 tbsp (45 mL) oat milk

1 tsp (5 mL) vanilla

2 tbsp (30 mL) finely chopped candied ginger

1 Preheat oven to 350°F (180°C) and lightly grease or line a 9-inch (23 cm) square baking pan with parchment paper.

2 CAKE: In a bowl, sift together flour, cocoa, salt, baking powder, baking soda and ginger; set aside.

3 In a large bowl, whisk together oat milk, eggs, brown sugar, oil, ginger and vanilla until smooth. Add the flour mixture to wet ingredients and mix until just combined. Spread batter into prepared pan, smoothing the top. Bake for 25 minutes, or until a tester inserted in the center comes out clean. Let cool in pan.

4 ICING: Into a medium bowl, sift confectioners' sugar and cocoa powder. Stir in oat milk and vanilla until smooth. Add more oat milk if you desire a thinner icing. Spread over cake, then sprinkle with candied ginger.

TIP

Instead of oat milk, use your favorite plant-based milk, such as nut, seed or soy milk.

SOUR CREAM PIE PASTRY

MAKES DOUGH FOR A DOUBLE CRUST PIE

Buttery, flaky, easy — all describe this food-processor pie crust!
You can enjoy using this recipe in our Jillian's Favorite Aussie Beef
Meat Pies (page 116), Apple Cranberry Sheet-Pan Pie (page 225)
and Salted Chocolate Pecan Tarts (page 226).

3 cups (750 mL)
all-purpose flour

1 tbsp (15 mL) granulated
sugar

1/2 tsp (2 mL) salt

1 cup (250 mL) butter,
cubed

1/3 cup (75 mL) vegetable
shortening, cubed

1/2 cup (125 mL) full-fat
sour cream

3 tbsp (45 mL) cold water

1 In a food processor, add flour, sugar and salt; pulse
to combine. Add butter and shortening and pulse
until crumbs are pea size. Add sour cream and
water. Pulse until the dough just comes together.

2 Remove dough from bowl and shape into two
rectangles. Wrap in plastic wrap and refrigerate
until firm, about 30 minutes.

TIP

This dough can be stored in the refrigerator for
up to 2 days or frozen for up to 3 months. If frozen,
let thaw in refrigerator overnight.

APPLE CRANBERRY SHEET-PAN PIE

SERVES 12 TO 16 · ·

Here's a delicious classic dessert that will please and feed your whole family. We've combined apples with tart dried cranberries and baked them in a standard quarter-sheet pan. Use an assortment of apples to get the best texture and flavor. The Sour Cream Pie Pastry is sturdy enough that the pie squares can be eaten by hand — no cutlery or plates required!

3½ lbs (1.75 kg) apples, peeled and cubed into ½-inch (1 cm) pieces

½ cup (125 mL) dried cranberries

½ cup (125 mL) packed brown sugar

¼ cup (60 mL) cornstarch

2 tbsp (30 mL) lemon juice

1½ tsp (7 mL) ground cinnamon

¼ tsp (1 mL) ground cloves

¼ tsp (1 mL) salt

1 recipe Sour Cream Pie Pastry (see page 224)

2 tbsp (30 mL) butter, cut into very small pieces

1 large egg

1 tsp (5 mL) milk

1 tbsp (15 mL) coarse sugar

1. In a large bowl, combine apples, cranberries, brown sugar, cornstarch, lemon juice, cinnamon, cloves and salt; toss to evenly coat; set aside.

2. Position oven rack in the lower third of oven. Preheat oven to 425°F (220°C). Set aside a 13- by 9-inch (33 by 23 cm) rimmed sheet pan.

3. On a lightly floured surface, roll out one half the pastry into a 16- by 12-inch (40 by 30 cm) rectangle. Gently fit pastry into sheet pan, pressing into corners. Evenly spread the apple filling on the pastry in pan, pressing gently to flatten; it will be full, but apples will cook down. Sprinkle butter pieces all over the top of filling.

4. On a lightly floured surface, roll the second half of pastry into a 15- by 11-inch (38 by 28 cm) rectangle. Drape over filling and fold the edge of the bottom dough over top dough. Pinch edges of pastry to seal. Using a sharp knife, make slits in the top pastry to allow steam to escape.

5. In a small bowl, beat the egg and milk, brush onto the crust, then sprinkle sugar on top. Bake for 10 minutes, then reduce oven temperature to 350°F (180°C) and bake for about 45 minutes or until crust is golden and apples are tender. Let cool about 2 hours before serving.

SALTED CHOCOLATE PECAN TARTS

SERVES 12 ·

We love pecan pie, so why not add a decadent twist with chocolate and make a mini version? These buttery treats have a sweet-salty flavor balance that is delicious. Make this dessert extra special and serve with a little scoop of ice cream or whipped cream. They're a perfect make-ahead for holiday celebrations.

1/2 cup (125 mL) packed brown sugar

1/4 cup (60 mL) butter, melted and slightly cooled

1/4 cup (60 mL) corn syrup

1 large egg

1 tsp (5 mL) cider vinegar

1 tsp (5 mL) vanilla

1/4 tsp (1 mL) salt

1/2 recipe Sour Cream Pie Pastry (see page 224)

1/2 cup (125 mL) dark chocolate chunks

1/2 cup (125 mL) chopped pecans

Maldon sea salt crystals or other coarse salt

1 Position oven rack in the lower third of oven. Preheat oven to 375°F (190°C). Set aside a 12-cup muffin tin.

2 In a medium bowl, whisk together brown sugar, butter, corn syrup, egg, vinegar, vanilla and salt until smooth; set aside.

3 On a lightly floured surface, roll out pastry to 1/4-inch (0.5 cm) thickness and cut out 12 rounds with a 4-inch (10 cm) cookie cutter, rerolling scraps as needed. Line each muffin cup with a piece of dough. Evenly divide chocolate chunks and pecans into each tart shell, then spoon the filling into each shell. Bake on bottom rack for about 18 to 20 minutes or until pastry is golden and filling is bubbly.

4 Remove from oven and sprinkle a little sea salt on top of each tart. Let cool completely in pan on a wire rack. Run a knife around the edges and carefully remove tarts from cups.

TIPS

Store tarts in a single layer in a shallow airtight container at room temperature for up to 4 days or freeze for up to 2 months.

If desired, toast the pecans in a small skillet, over medium heat, until lightly browned and fragrant, about 2 to 3 minutes. Transfer to a bowl to cool before using.

For a shortcut, use store-bought pastry for a 9-inch (23 cm) single-crust pie.

BUMBLEBERRY CRUMB CAKE

SERVES 9 ·

Under a tender crumb topping and a layer of colorful berries, you'll find a scrumptious buttery cake. Although this cake is in our Sweets chapter, we do love it for breakfast and tea time. The cake is beautiful as is, but you can dress it up with a simple dusting of powdered sugar.

TOPPING

1/2 cup (125 mL)
  all-purpose flour

1/4 cup (60 mL) packed
  light brown sugar

1/4 cup (60 mL) butter,
  melted

1/4 cup (60 mL) chopped
  walnuts or pecans

1/4 tsp (1 mL) salt

CAKE

1 1/2 cups (375 mL)
  all-purpose flour

1 tsp (5 mL) baking powder

1/2 tsp (2 mL) salt

1/4 tsp (1 mL) baking soda

3/4 cup (175 mL) granulated
  sugar

2 large eggs

3/4 cup (175 mL) full-fat
  plain yogurt or sour
  cream

1/2 cup (125 mL) canola oil

1 tsp (5 mL) grated lemon
  zest

1 1/2 tsp (7 mL) vanilla

1 1/2 cups (375 mL) mixed
  fresh or frozen berries,
  divided

1 Preheat oven to 350°F (180°C) and line a 9-inch (23 cm) square baking pan with parchment paper.

2 TOPPING: In a small bowl, combine flour, brown sugar, butter, walnuts and salt, stir to combine; set aside.

3 CAKE: In a medium bowl, whisk together flour, baking powder, salt and baking soda; set aside. In a large bowl, using an electric mixer, combine sugar, eggs, yogurt, oil, lemon zest and vanilla until smooth. Add flour mixture to wet ingredients and mix until just combined. Use a spatula to gently fold in half of the berries. Spread batter into prepared pan and sprinkle the remaining berries on top. Sprinkle topping over cake. Bake for 40 to 45 minutes, or until a tester inserted in the center comes out clean. Let cool in pan on wire rack.

TIPS

The topping can be prepared up to 2 days ahead. Store in an airtight container in the refrigerator until ready to use.

The cake can be stored at room temperature in an airtight container at room temperature for up to 3 days or in the freezer for 1 month.

If using frozen berries, do not thaw them before adding.

STRAWBERRY SHORTCAKES

SERVES 12

These cakes are light and moist but still a bit heavier than a sponge-style cake. Crushing the strawberries and using them as a sauce for the filling instead of having traditional sliced berries is a wonderful variation on a classic.

2½ cups (625 mL) all-purpose flour

¼ cup (60 mL) packed light brown sugar

1 tbsp (15 mL) baking powder

1 tsp (5 mL) grated orange zest

¼ tsp (1 mL) salt

¾ cup (175 mL) butter, cubed

1 cup (250 mL) milk (approx.)

2 cups (500 mL) whole hulled fresh strawberries, crushed

Small fresh whole strawberries

Fresh mint leaves

VANILLA WHIPPED CREAM

1¼ cups (310 mL) heavy or whipping (35%) cream

2 tbsp (30 mL) packed light brown sugar

1 tsp (5 mL) vanilla

1 In a large bowl, combine flour, brown sugar, baking powder, orange zest and salt. Using pastry blender or fingertips, cut in butter until mixture resembles coarse crumbs. Add milk all at once, stirring with fork to make soft, slightly sticky dough.

2 On lightly floured surface, knead dough gently about 10 times to bring dough together. Pat dough into ½-inch (1 cm) thick round. Using floured 3-inch (7.5 cm) round cookie cutter, cut out rounds. Place on parchment paper lined baking sheet. Gather scraps, pat out again and cut to make a total of 12 rounds.

3 Lightly brush tops of biscuits with some more milk. Bake in 425°F (220°C) oven for about 12 minutes or until bottom is golden. Let cool to room temperature. Cut each biscuit in half crosswise.

4 VANILLA WHIPPED CREAM: Meanwhile, in a bowl, whip cream, brown sugar and vanilla to smooth, stiff peaks; set aside. Spoon crushed strawberries over bottom halves of each biscuit. Dollop with whipped cream and top with remaining biscuit halves. Garnish tops with more cream, small strawberry and mint leaves.

MAKE AHEAD

Just cover the assembled shortcakes and refrigerate for up to 1 day. Let them come to room temperature before eating.

TIP

Crush strawberries using a potato masher in a shallow dish in a single layer. Drizzle the juice onto the shortcakes before spooning crushed berries onto bottom layer.

EASY LEMON SEMIFREDDO WITH BLUEBERRY SAUCE

SERVES 10 ·

No matter how full you are after dinner, you're going to want to make room for this make-ahead winning dessert. Semifreddo means semi-frozen. It's a little rich and decadent with a luscious blueberry sauce to complement the lemon. This smooth and creamy treat is quick to make using the convenience of prepared lemon curd.

SEMIFREDDO

$1^3/_4$ cups (425 mL) heavy or whipping (35%) cream

1 jar (12 oz/340 g) lemon curd (about $1^1/_4$ cups/ 300 mL)

BLUEBERRY SAUCE

2 cups (500 mL) blueberries (fresh or frozen)

$1/_2$ cup (125 mL) water

$1/_4$ cup (60 mL) granulated sugar

3 tbsp (45 mL) lemon juice

1 tbsp (15 mL) cornstarch

2 tsp (10 mL) grated lemon zest

1 SEMIFREDDO: Line a 9- by 5-inch (23 by 12.5 cm) loaf pan with a large double layer of plastic wrap, leaving a 4-inch (10 cm) overhang along the sides. In a large bowl, using an electric hand mixer, whip cream until soft peaks form. Using a spatula, gently fold in the lemon curd. Pour mixture into prepared pan, smooth top, fold overhanging plastic wrap over the top and freeze overnight.

2 BLUEBERRY SAUCE: In a medium pot, over medium heat, combine blueberries, water and sugar; bring to a boil, then reduce heat to low. In a small bowl, whisk together lemon juice and cornstarch; gently stir into blueberries. Let simmer gently for 2 minutes; mixture will thicken. Remove from heat and stir in lemon zest. (Makes 2 cups/500 mL.)

3 To serve, unfold plastic wrap, flip semifreddo onto serving plate, lift loaf pan and remove plastic. Let stand a minute or two for loaf to soften slightly for easier slicing. Drizzle blueberry sauce on top of loaf for a beautiful presentation. You can also place slices on serving plates, then drizzle blueberry sauce over each serving.

MAKE AHEAD

Semifreddo can be frozen for up to 2 weeks.

Blueberry sauce keeps well in the refrigerator for up to 5 days. Mixture will have thickened. Reheat gently to thin sauce, adding a little water if necessary.

MANGO WHITE CHOCOLATE CHEESECAKE CUPS

SERVES 14 ·

This cheesecake cup has a light mousse-like texture and looks so inviting with a bit of mango swirled into the top of each cheesecake. It freezes well, which makes it perfect for snacking in the future or a dessert at the last minute.

CRUST

1 cup (250 mL) graham wafer crumbs

1/4 cup (60 mL) unsweetened flaked coconut

3 tbsp (45 mL) butter, melted

1 tbsp (15 mL) granulated sugar

FILLING

8 oz (250 g) brick-style cream cheese, softened

6 oz (175 g) white chocolate, melted

1 1/2 cups (375 mL) canned mango purée, divided

2 tbsp (30 mL) lemon juice

3/4 cup (175 mL) heavy or whipping (35%) cream

GARNISHES (OPTIONAL)

Fresh mango, toasted coconut and white chocolate shavings

1 CRUST: In a bowl, stir together wafer crumbs, coconut, butter and sugar; mix well to combine. Evenly divide the crumb mixture into 14 mini mason jars or 1/2 cup (125 mL) ramekins and gently pack down with the back of a spoon.

2 FILLING: In a large bowl, using an electric mixer, beat cream cheese until lightened. Beat in white chocolate until smooth. Set aside 2 tbsp (30 mL) of mango purée to be used for garnish. Add remaining mango and lemon juice; beat until smooth.

3 In another bowl, using clean beaters, whip cream to soft peaks. Fold in half of the whipped cream into the mango mixture; gently mix to combine. Fold in remaining whipped cream until smooth.

4 Evenly divide mixture into each jar. Spoon about 1/2 teaspoon (2 mL) of remaining mango onto the top of each jar. Using a toothpick or skewer, gently stir the surface to create a swirled pattern on top. Cover each with a lid or plastic wrap. Chill overnight. Garnish with fresh mango, toasted coconut and white chocolate shavings, if desired.

TIP
Refrigerate for up to 3 days. Can be frozen for up to 1 month.

STRAWBERRY RHUBARB COBBLER

SERVES 8 TO 10

Add a splash of rum or vanilla to whipped cream to serve with this summertime favorite. Be sure to celebrate the short rhubarb season or use up last year's harvest from the freezer!

3 cups (750 mL) chopped fresh or frozen rhubarb

2 cups (500 mL) sliced fresh or frozen strawberries

1 1/2 cups (375 mL) granulated sugar, divided

2 tbsp (30 mL) cornstarch

1/3 cup (75 mL) butter, melted

1 cup (250 mL) all-purpose flour

1 1/2 tsp (7 mL) baking powder

1/4 tsp (1 mL) salt

3/4 cup (175 mL) milk

TOPPING

2 tbsp (30 mL) granulated sugar

1/2 tsp (2 mL) ground cinnamon

1/4 tsp (1 mL) grated nutmeg

1. In a saucepan, combine rhubarb, strawberries, 3/4 cup (175 mL) of the sugar and cornstarch over medium heat and cook, stirring until sugar is dissolved and mixture thickens. Set aside.

2. Preheat oven to 350°F (180°C). Pour melted butter into a lightly sprayed 13- by 9-inch (33 by 23 cm) baking dish.

3. In a bowl, whisk together flour, remaining sugar, baking powder and salt. Stir in milk until just combined. Pour batter into pan with melted butter and smooth into an even layer. Do not stir in butter.

4. Spoon fruit mixture over top of the batter.

5. TOPPING: In a small bowl, stir together sugar, cinnamon and nutmeg. Sprinkle over top of fruit and bake for about 35 minutes or until cake is golden. Let cool slightly before serving.

PEACH MELBA TIRAMISU

MAKES 14 SERVINGS ·

Traditional tiramisu is made with coffee and mascarpone cheese. Our twist on this classic dessert uses fresh peaches and raspberries, with lady fingers dipped in peach nectar. This recipe feeds a crowd and is perfect for easy summer entertaining.

4 cups (1 L) chopped ripe, peeled peaches

4 cups (1 L) fresh raspberries

2 tbsp (30 mL) lemon juice

2 packages (8 oz/250 g) brick-style cream cheese, softened

1/2 cup (125 mL) confectioners' (icing) sugar

2 tsp (10 mL) vanilla

3 cups (750 mL) heavy or whipping (35%) cream

1 1/4 cups (300 mL) peach nectar

2 tsp (10 mL) grated lemon zest

3 tbsp (45 mL) peach or orange liqueur

14 oz (400 g) lady finger biscuits

1 In a large bowl, gently combine peaches, raspberries and lemon juice; set aside.

2 In a bowl of an electric stand mixer, using whip attachment, beat cream cheese, confectioners' sugar and vanilla on medium speed until smooth, about 2 minutes; scrape down sides occasionally. Continue beating and slowly drizzle in heavy cream; scrape down sides occasionally. Beat until creamy and fluffy.

3 In a small bowl, combine peach nectar, lemon zest and peach liqueur; set aside. In a 13- by 9-inch (33 by 23 cm) glass baking dish, place one layer of lady fingers. Drizzle half of the nectar mixture over top. Sprinkle half of the fruit mixture on top, then evenly spread half of the cream mixture on top. Repeat layers with remaining ingredients. Cover and refrigerate for at least 6 hours or overnight before serving.

TIPS

Store any leftovers in the refrigerator for up to 2 days.

Fresh peaches can be substituted with 1 can (796 mL/28 oz) peaches.

For a family-friendly version, substitute the liqueur with 3 tbsp (45 mL) peach nectar.

CHOCOLATE PEANUT BUTTER MOUSSE PIE

SERVES 8 TO 10 ·

Our good friend and fellow cookbook author Jennifer MacKenzie put this classic combination of chocolate and peanut butter together for a decadently light pie you cannot resist!

CRUST

1½ cups (375 mL) chocolate wafer crumbs

¼ cup (60 mL) butter, melted

GANACHE

4 oz (125 g) 70% bittersweet chocolate, chopped

½ cup (125 mL) heavy or whipping (35%) cream

PEANUT BUTTER MOUSSE

¾ cup (175 mL) smooth peanut butter

1½ cups (375 mL) heavy or whipping (35%) cream

2 tbsp (30 mL) granulated sugar

½ tsp (2 mL) vanilla

1 Preheat oven to 350°F (180°C).

2 CRUST: In a bowl, stir together crumbs and butter until well moistened. Press into bottom and sides of a 9-inch (23 cm) pie plate. Bake for about 8 minutes, or until firm. Let cool.

3 GANACHE: Place chocolate in a bowl. In a small saucepan, bring cream just to boil over medium heat. Or heat in microwave in 30-second intervals until steaming. Pour over chocolate, stirring until melted. Pour half into bottom prepared crust and carefully spread evenly.

4 PEANUT BUTTER MOUSSE: In a bowl over saucepan of hot (not boiling) water, melt peanut butter; let cool slightly. Meanwhile, in another bowl, whip cream, sugar and vanilla to stiff peaks. Fold one quarter into peanut butter until blended. Gently fold in remaining whipped cream until well combined.

5 Spoon mousse into crust and smooth the top. Drizzle or dollop with remaining ganache and swirl with a skewer, if desired. Refrigerate for at least 4 hours or, alternatively, place in freezer for at least 4 hours or until firm. Let thaw slightly if frozen before serving.

TIP

Cover in plastic wrap and foil to leave in freezer for up to 2 weeks before thawing to serve.

STICKY TOFFEE PUDDING

SERVES 12

This lovely light cake smothered with butterscotch sauce means you can serve up a restaurant favorite at home.

STICKY TOFFEE PUDDING

1 cup (250 mL) water

1 cup (250 mL) chopped pitted Medjool dates

1/4 cup (60 mL) butter, softened

2/3 cup (150 mL) packed light brown sugar

2 large eggs

2 tsp (10 mL) vanilla

1 1/3 cups (325 mL) all-purpose flour

1 tbsp (15 mL) baking powder

1 tsp (5 mL) baking soda

BUTTERSCOTCH SAUCE

1/2 cup (125 mL) butter

1 1/2 cups (375 mL) packed light brown sugar

2/3 cup (150 mL) heavy or whipping (35%) cream

1/4 cup (60 mL) Rogers or Lyle's golden syrup or corn syrup

1 STICKY TOFFEE PUDDING: In a saucepan, bring water and dates to a simmer. Cover and simmer for 2 minutes; set aside to cool.

2 Preheat oven to 350°F (180°C). Line an 8- by 4-inch (20 by 10 cm) loaf pan with parchment paper; set aside.

3 Meanwhile, in a large bowl, beat butter and brown sugar until fluffy. Beat in eggs, one at a time, beating well after each addition. Beat in vanilla.

2 In another bowl, whisk together flour, baking powder and soda. Stir into butter mixture until well combined. Stir in cooled date mixture until no streaks remain. Spread into prepared pan. Bake for about 35 minutes or until tester inserted in center comes out clean. Let cool in pan on rack for about 15 minutes before turning out to serve.

3 BUTTERSCOTCH SAUCE: In a saucepan, bring butter, brown sugar, cream and golden syrup to boil over medium heat. Reduce heat and simmer, stirring occasionally for 3 minutes.

4 Slice toffee pudding and spoon sauce over each slice to serve.

MUFFIN-SIZE VARIATION

Divide batter into 12 greased muffin tins and bake for about 20 minutes or until tester inserted in center comes out clean.

ALMOND CELEBRATION CAKE

SERVES 16 TO 20 ·

Showcase your love of sweets with this buttery vanilla cake and buttercream icing for anyone's special celebration! This cake is an inspiration from an old restaurant that Emily remembers as a kid. Family members would ask for "The Knotty Pine" butter cake. What a wonderful flavor memory to have!

CELEBRATION CAKE

2³/₄ cups (675 mL) all-purpose flour

2 tsp (10 mL) baking powder

¹/₂ tsp (2 mL) baking soda

¹/₄ tsp (1 mL) salt

1 cup (250 mL) 2% milk

1 cup (250 mL) sour cream

4 tsp (20 mL) vanilla

1 cup (250 mL) butter, softened

1¹/₂ cups (375 mL) granulated sugar

4 large eggs, at room temperature

ALMOND BUTTERCREAM

1¹/₂ cups (375 mL) butter, softened

6 cups (1.5 L) confectioners' (icing) sugar

1 cup (250 mL) heavy or whipping (35%) cream

1 tbsp (15 mL) almond extract

¹/₂ cup (125 mL) sliced almonds, toasted

1 Butter or spray two 8-inch (20 cm) springform or 2-inch (5 cm) high cake pans and line bottoms with parchment paper. Preheat oven to 350°F (180°C).

2 CAKE: In a bowl, whisk together flour, baking powder, baking soda and salt; set aside. In a small bowl, whisk together milk, sour cream and vanilla.

3 In a large bowl, using a stand or handheld mixer, beat butter and sugar until smooth. Beat in eggs one at a time, then beat mixture for about 2 minutes or until light colored and very fluffy. Stir in ¹/₃ of the flour mixture, then ¹/₂ of the milk mixture; repeat once, ending with remaining flour. Stir until well combined.

4 Pour batter equally into prepared pans and smooth tops. Bake for about 35 minutes or until light golden all over and tester inserted in center comes out clean. Let cool in pan on rack for 20 minutes, then turn out onto rack and remove parchment paper. Let cool completely.

5 BUTTERCREAM: Meanwhile, in a large bowl, using stand or handheld mixer, beat butter until very light in color. Slowly beat in half of the confectioners' sugar. Add cream and almond extract and beat until combined. Beat in remaining sugar until light and fluffy. Set aside at room temperature.

6 Turn cakes over and, using a long serrated knife, trim cake top to level if necessary. Cut each cake in half to get four even layers. Place one layer on cake stand or board and spread with a generous $1/2$ cup (125 mL) of the buttercream. Repeat with remaining layers. Spread some of the buttercream all around the cake to create a thin layer of buttercream, which will set the crumbs. Refrigerate cake for at least 1 hour or until buttercream is firm and set. (Keep remaining buttercream at room temperature, simply cover with plastic wrap.)

7 Remove cake from fridge and spread with remaining buttercream and decorate with almonds as desired. Refrigerate up to 2 days ahead. Let come to room temperature before cutting to serve.

VANILLA VARIATION

Omit almond extract in icing and substitute vanilla. Omit almonds, if desired.

TIPS

Make this cake your own and add your favorite sprinkles on the inside and outside! If you want a little fruit flavor, spread some of your favorite thick jam on the cake layers before you add the icing.

Make sure the cakes are completely cooled before icing to prevent the cakes from sinking from the weight of the layers.

If you don't have high-sided pans, you can use four cake pans that are 1 inch (2.5 cm) high instead.

Make sure all of your pans are the same size and made from the same material. If they are different, keep an eye on them, as they may bake at slightly different times. Darker pans may cook more quickly, and heavier pans may need extra baking time.

Library and Archives Canada Cataloguing in Publication

Title: Best of Bridge everyday celebrations : 125 recipes for friends & family.

Other titles: Everyday celebrations

Names: Kong, Sylvia, author. | Richards, Emily, author.

Description: Written by Sylvia Kong and Emily Richards. | Includes index.

Identifiers: Canadiana 20220206422 | ISBN 9780778807087 (hardcover)

Subjects: LCSH: Cooking. | LCSH: Entertaining. | LCGFT: Cookbooks.

Classification: LCC TX714 .K66 2022 | DDC 641.5—dc23

Why couldn't Sylvia and Emily's teddy bears finish their dessert? Because they were stuffed.

INDEX